Special Educational Nee⊔ and School Improvement

Special Educational Needs and School Improvement

Practical Strategies for Raising Standards

JEAN GROSS AND ANGELA WHITE

David Fulton Publishers

London

David Fulton Publishers Ltd
The Chiswick Centre, 414 Chiswick High Road, London W4 5TF

www.fultonpublishers.co.uk

David Fulton Publishers is a division of Granada Learning Limited, part of the Granada Media Group

First published in 2003

10 9 8 7 6 5 4 3 2 1

British Library Cataloguing in Publication Data
A catalogue record for this book is available from the British Library

ISBN 1–84312–011–9

Typeset by Mark Heslington, Scarborough, North Yorkshire
Printed and bound in Great Britain by Ashford Colour Press, Gosport, Hants.

Contents

Acknowledgements

We are grateful to a number of outstanding SENCOs and former SENCOs:

Ginny Campbell, at Kingsbridge Community College, Devon, for her account of a very effective whole-school approach to reducing bureaucracy and improving communication systems;

Mike Parsons, Hengrove School, Bristol, for permission to include the information leaflet about the school's inclusion provision which he has developed for parents and carers;

Shirley Stevenson, at St George Community College, Bristol, for her work on provision mapping and criteria for accessing additional support in the secondary school; and

Sue Derrington, Bristol LEA, for her work on criteria for accessing support in the primary school.

Particular thanks go to Ann Berger, HMI, an inspirational former colleague with whom many of the ideas in this book were first developed.

Introduction: how to use this book

This is a book for head teachers, SENCOs, school governors, LEA inclusion managers and support services, LEA advisers, registered inspectors and lecturers in higher education. Its aim is to help mainstream schools raise the attainment and promote the inclusion of pupils with special educational needs (SEN), by applying to SEN the tools for school improvement which have proved successful in raising standards for the broad majority of pupils. It will enable experienced managers (and those who support them) to apply to SEN key principles and processes with which they are already familiar, but may not have thought about in an SEN context.

It will also, for some readers – such as SENCOs who have not been included within senior management teams – introduce some of these principles and processes for the first time, and suggest to them a potential role as a strategic manager rather than a manager only of Individual Education Plans (IEPs), paperwork and meetings.

The book can be used in a number of ways:

- a straightforward 'read';
- a source of practical tools – proformas, checklists, audit documents; or
- a course text to accompany an in-service training programme, materials for which are provided in the Appendix at the end of the book.

As a course text, it is suitable for:

- head teachers and other senior managers on leadership programmes;
- award-bearing courses for SENCOs, linked to the Teacher Training Agency (TTA) SENCO standards;
- short courses for SENCOs, focusing on their management role; or
- governor training.

1 Why plan strategically for SEN?

Introduction

Books on special educational needs traditionally focus on the nature of individual children's SEN and how to address them. Much has been written, also, on the systems involved in the SEN Code of Practice – IEPs, SMART targets, parental involvement, pupil involvement and other essentially process-oriented and operational themes.

This book is different. It is about how to manage SEN strategically, rather than operationally; it is about managing SEN at a whole-school level, as part of a school's overall school improvement process, rather than about meeting the needs of individuals.

It is about applying to SEN the familiar school improvement questions (DfEE/QCA 2001):

- How well are we doing?
- How do we compare with similar schools?
- How well should we be doing?
- What more should we aim to achieve next year?
- What must we do to make it happen?

The model used is a cyclical one and looks like this:

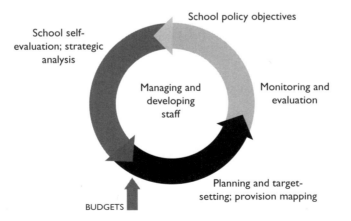

Figure 1.1 The school improvement cycle

It begins with setting some broad **policy objectives**, based on the school's vision for what it wants to achieve for children with SEN, alongside what it wants to achieve for other vulnerable groups within the wider educational inclusion umbrella.

The next step is **evaluation and strategic analysis**:

- answering the question 'How well are we doing?' in relation to those policy objectives by using a range of quantitative and qualitative tools, which include seeking the views of children and parents/carers;
- using data to answer the questions 'How do we compare with similar schools?' and 'How well should we be doing?';
- looking to the future and the broader context of SEN within education; answering the questions 'What's out there?', 'What changes are going on in the environment and how might they affect us?'; and
- gathering information about the future profile of SEN within the school: 'How many children?' 'With what types of need?' 'In what year groups?'

After evaluation comes **planning and target setting**: answering the questions 'What more should we aim to achieve next year? and 'What must we do to make it happen?' For SEN, this will be a dual process: establishing priorities for the SEN element of the School Improvement Plan (setting improvement targets and planning actions) and simultaneously planning the actual provision which the school will put in place for the coming year in the form of additional adult support.

The next stage is **implementation** of planning and provision, with the focus on monitoring and evaluating the implementation of plans in classrooms, and the impact on children's progress.

After implementation comes evaluation, as the cycle begins again.

At the heart of the whole cyclical process is **managing and developing staff**: the ongoing school systems for helping all staff to evaluate their own practice, learn from one another and from outside, and develop as professionals.

What's new about managing SEN strategically?

Many schools have found it difficult to apply the questions 'How well are we doing?' and 'How do we compare with similar schools?' to SEN. At a national level, systems for measuring the attainment and progress of children with SEN in agreed ways which allow for comparisons between schools are still embryonic; use of the 'P' scales (DfEE/QCA 2001) is not universal in mainstream schools, and little analysis is done of data that is already available, such as the percentage of pupils attaining at the lower National Curriculum levels at end-of-key stage assessment.

There are deeper reasons for the lack of use of data on pupils with SEN, however. One reason relates to an emphasis in the SEN world on providing **support** for children with SEN, rather than on the outcomes of that support. The majority of SEN effort in schools and LEAs goes on the complex systems for identifying need and proving (or disproving) the case for additional help

(Ofsted/Audit Commission 2002). The goal at school level is often that the child will be allocated funding, and therefore enabled to remain in the classroom with his or her peer group without placing too great a demand on the class or subject teacher. The support, once allocated, is usually long-term; it is more often targeted at 'coaxing the child to comply with the inappropriate curriculum on offer' (Gross 2000) than, for example, ensuring that the child attains a certain level in the end-of-key stage assessments.

Much SEN work, then, is about support for individual children, and the processes of the SEN Code of Practice which enable them to access support. There is a degree of focus on outcomes, as defined in Individual Education Plan targets, but these are particular to the child and do not allow for any comparison between schools. They allow schools to answer the question 'How are we doing for David?', but not 'How are we doing for children with SEN in general; for children with behavioural, emotional and social needs; for children with SEN in Key Stage 3; in literacy; in mathematics?'

Because of this, schools are not able to set themselves targets for improvement. They can only set targets for improvement for David. Although the law requires that the governing body reports annually to parents on the implementation of the school's SEN policy, relatively few schools have set measurable targets which would enable them to report in this way (Thomas and Tarr 1996). Where they have, these are usually about the percentage of children moving 'down' from School Action Plus to School Action or to the normal differentiated curriculum – the only statistic which schools reliably gather.

Yet simple measures *do* exist which schools can use to set targets, and some LEAs have been able to supply schools with information allowing them to compare their own performance with that of similar schools. Chapter 3 of this book will give examples of this approach.

A further reason for the emphasis in SEN on the operational rather than the strategic is the sheer complexity of the processes involved, with their quasi-legalistic overtones and quasi-medical approach to diagnosing needs and prescribing remedies. It is this which makes many of those who have had training in strategic management (usually head teachers or aspiring head teachers) to steer clear of applying their knowledge about strategic planning to SEN. They feel de-skilled by its complexities, and by the volume of paperwork it generates. The temptation is to leave those complexities to the person who is often least likely to have had training in strategic management but does know her or his Code of Practice, the SENCO. In these circumstances, a team approach can be lacking.

Again, this is not difficult to remedy; all it takes is a little less anxiety among senior managers about the mystique of SEN, a little more time and status for the SENCO and a realisation that SEN is as amenable to improvement as any other of the school's spheres of operation. It also takes some tools, and this is what this book aims to provide.

Why manage SEN strategically?

The first argument for applying school improvement processes to SEN is one of equity. Where schools feel driven by the national targets for the attainment of the broad majority of children, and for the more able, it makes sense to set school-level targets also for those who have difficulties in learning. Targets, preceded by self-evaluation and followed by actions that are carefully planned and monitored, do work: we have only to look at the increase in the number of children reaching nationally expected levels at the end of their key stage or at the (short-lived) reduction in permanent exclusions during the period when targets were set in this area to see this. Planning strategically at whole-school level for children with SEN is thus likely to mean that they make better progress and improve their life chances.

A second reason for adopting a strategic approach is the impact this is likely to have on the attainment and progress of children who do not have SEN. At a crude level, taking resolute action to reduce the percentage of children who fail to acquire very basic literacy or numeracy skills before they leave the primary school will make classes easier to teach: the learning of the majority can be all too easily disrupted by the behaviours that stem from the frustration and low self-esteem of those who are not making progress, and who know it.

Less crudely, there is increasing evidence (for example, Wilce 2001) that schools which have focused their school improvement planning on increasing their capacity to include all children, via appropriate staff development and resource allocation, will, as a result, raise attainment across the board. The reasons for this are not hard to see: for every child with complex SEN for whom a teacher learns to make specific adaptations to curriculum delivery there are likely to be several more in the class with lesser needs, who benefit equally – from greater clarity in the teacher's use of language, for example, or from the use of alternatives to traditional paper and pencil recording, or from class work on how to handle arguments and defuse conflict.

Finally, there are a number of 'external' reasons which may encourage schools to embrace lower-attaining pupils in their regular school improvement processes. The main external frameworks for monitoring and accountability now focus sharply on the achievement and participation of all. Ofsted, for example, expects effective schools to have analysed the data on different groups of pupils (including those with SEN), and to set clear targets based on their analysis. The inspection focus has shifted attention increasingly onto the performance of vulnerable children, rather than exclusively on those who do not experience barriers to their learning.

Similarly, the trend towards greater delegation of SEN funding to schools, accompanied by a stronger monitoring role for LEAs, is likely to mean that schools who can show that they are evaluating their own performance with children who have SEN will be well placed to demonstrate their effective use of resources. They will also, if they use information such as that presented in Chapter 7 of this book on 'what works?' in different possible interventions for pupils with SEN, be able to demonstrate that they have applied Best Value principles to their job of raising attainment and promoting inclusion for all.

2 How to plan strategically for SEN

STEP ONE: agree your school policy objectives

The first step in being strategic about SEN is having a clear sense, as a school, of what you want to achieve **as an outcome** for children who experience difficulties in learning.

The simplest way to define the outcomes you want to achieve is to discuss, as a staff, how you would complete the sentence 'We make

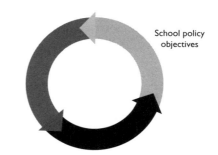

Figure 2.1 The school improvement cycle

provision in this school for children with SEN in order that . . .'. The answers may be varied; for example:

- . . . in order that every child can reach his or her potential;
- . . . in order to develop pupils' self-esteem and confidence;
- . . . in order that all children can access the curriculum;
- . . . in order that all children leave our school with the core skills (such as literacy, numeracy, personal organisation and social independence) they will need in adult life;
- . . . in order to raise the attainment of all pupils;
- . . . in order that all children can be included fully within their peer group; and
- . . . in order to help all children learn the social, emotional and behavioural competencies they need in order to sustain positive relationships with others.

The sentence completions will generally focus on three areas: attainment; achievement, in the broader sense (including personal and social achievement); and inclusion. Because of this it may be possible to combine them into a single, succinct statement such as 'Our objectives are to raise attainment and promote inclusion.'

It is necessary to spend a little time clarifying the school's broad objectives in order that these can then be used to generate ways in which progress towards them can be measured – that is by setting SMART (specific, measurable, achievable, realistic, time-constrained) targets, like those on IEPs.

Some definitions of broad objectives lend themselves more readily to generating measurable targets than others. For example, the objective 'Our aim is for all children to reach their potential' might be difficult; how would the school know (and be able to measure) whether it was meeting its aim? In many primary schools the only measurement of children's 'potential' sits in teachers' heads, and is often either self-fulfilling, with low expectations leading to low attainment (Barber 1996; Blatchford *et al.* 1989) or just plain wrong. Secondary schools may define potential through CAT scores on entry to the school, which generate predicted attainment levels at Key Stages 3 and 4, but the same arguments hold about self-fulfilling prophecies, and there remain many debates about the validity of any sort of measurement of cognitive ability as a true predictor of what adults or children will achieve in life. Again, CAT scores measure only a limited range of 'potential': we are not yet at the stage of assessing all the intelligences (musical, linguistic, spatial, bodily-kinaesthetic, interpersonal and intrapersonal) which have been postulated (Gardner 1993) as central to achievement in its widest sense.

Other definitions of school policy objectives lend themselves more readily to generating measurable targets. 'Raising attainment', for example, might lead to a target to increase the percentage of children attaining at least level 1 at the end of Key Stage 1, at least level 3 at the end of Key Stage 2 or at least level 4 at the end of Key Stage 3. Such targets use data already available to the school.

In between these two extremes there is a third group of objectives which generate targets that can be measured, but require a little more effort. To set a target related to the objective that 'all children are included fully within their peer group', for example, the school would first need to define what that inclusion within the peer group would look like in practice, then find a way of gathering information year on year. They might decide, for example, to conduct some playground observations using an observation tool devised in conjunction with their educational psychologist to assess the extent to which children with complex needs were included in activities, rather than isolated. They might interview children themselves, using a semi-structured interview, to ask about their perceptions of the extent to which all children were included in friendship groups. Or they might use a more formal tool like a sociogram to look at choices within a class of 'who I like to work/play with'.

Such explorations often yield highly meaningful information: too many of them, however, may mean that the school experiences the process of target-setting for SEN as over-complex, and gives up on good intentions.

It is best, then, to make sure that the broad policy objectives which you agree as a whole school lead to a mixture of easy-to-measure and harder-to-measure (but possibly more meaningful) targets.

STEP TWO: evaluate how you are doing

The next step in the strategic management process is finding out what progress you have made towards meeting your agreed policy objectives, and finding out how well the school is doing compared to similar schools. The questions to ask yourself here are:

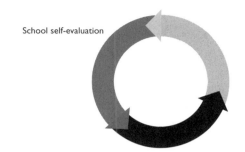

Figure 2.2 The school improvement cycle

- How well are we doing in relation to our policy objectives and linked targets?;
- How do we compare with similar schools?; and
- How well should we be doing?

Answering these questions requires a process of school self-evaluation, both qualitative and quantitative. The self-evaluation process is described in detail in Chapter 3 of this book.

STEP THREE: do a strategic analysis

In step three you ask the questions:

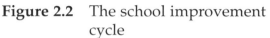

- What's out there? – looking to the future and to the broader national and local context;
- What is the profile of special educational need we will be meeting in the future?

Figure 2.3 The school improvement cycle

In asking these questions you will be taking stock of national and local policy directions and priorities in the area of SEN and inclusion. This stocktaking plays a key role in the *strategic* decisions which managers have to make about the direction in which the school will move in the medium to long term. The choice of direction in turn influences:

- the allocation of resources; and
- the areas for development to be pursued through changes to organisational structures, staff training and other forms of professional development.

Strategic decisions are taken following a process of strategic analysis. The process looks like this:

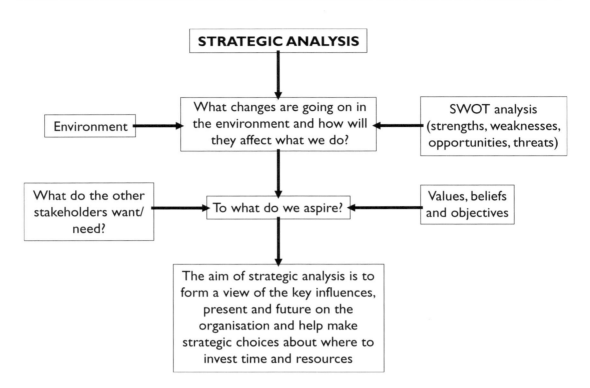

Figure 2.4 The process of strategic analysis

It is essential that SENCOs play a key part in the process of strategic analysis. Their role includes keeping up to date with what is happening in SEN at local and national level. It may also be useful to involve an external agency, such as a local SEN support service, or an educational psychologist at this point, as they may be able to bring a wider perspective, with knowledge of trends and initiatives of which the school may not be aware.

National priorities

At a national level, SEN priorities and policies have been set out in a number of key documents, notably the *Programme of Action* (DfEE 1998), the revised *SEN Code of Practice* (DfES 2001a) the *Inclusive Schooling* circular (DfES 2001b), and the *Accessible Schools* circular (DfES 2002a). The themes in these documents, and their implications for schools' strategic planning, are summarised in Table 2.1.

In turn, these SEN priorities are located within a broader national social inclusion agenda, with key documents such as *Evaluating Educational Inclusion* (Ofsted 2001) providing a definition of an educationally inclusive school and making clear that schools are expected to secure the full participation of pupils deemed, for a variety of reasons, to be 'at risk'.

Table 2.1 Implications of national policies and priorities for schools'
strategic planning

National policy: school-based responsibilities	Strategic implications for schools
Increasing delegation of SEN resources to school level; reduction in numbers of Statements of SEN; most children have their needs met at School Action or School Action Plus.	May need to change the way the school plans its staffing for SEN – opportunity to plan on a long-term basis against predictable levels of need, rather than on a short-term basis on the basis of individual children's funding allocations (see Chapter 6).
Clarification by LEAs of the provision which schools are expected to make; increase of external monitoring of use of resources/ outcomes for pupils with SEN.	Need to demonstrate clearly to parents and LEA the provision the school makes (see Chapter 6). Need to develop school-based self-evaluation of use of resources/outcomes, involving governors more actively in monitoring SEN provision (see Chapter 3).
Possible reduction in LEA SEN support services.	May need to invest in staff training so as to provide in-school expertise where it is no longer available from outside agencies.
National policy: early intervention	**Strategic implications for schools**
Increased emphasis on identifying children's needs early in their school career.	Need to consider screening systems for identifying need early.
Increased emphasis on Early Years Action and Early Years Action Plus, and intervening early in primary or secondary phase.	In the context of increased delegation of SEN funding to school level, may be able to alter patterns of provision so as to prioritise younger pupils.
National policy: parental involvement	**Strategic implications for schools**
Expectation that all parents of children with SEN should feel that they are treated as equal partners in decisions about their children.	May need to plan for staff training in communicating with parents.
Parent Partnership schemes in every LEA, supporting parents at School Action and School Action Plus as well as during process of statutory assessment/implementation and review of a Statement.	May need to plan to increase parental participation in assessment and planning.
Greater role for parents in holding schools to account for the provision they make for SEN.	May need to plan to improve communication with parents about the provision made in school, and the criteria for accessing the provision.
National policy: pupil involvement	**Strategic implications for schools**
Emphasis on rights of all children and young people with SEN to be involved in making decisions and exercising choice.	Need to review systems in school for involving pupils – school council, circle time forum for all, children helping to set individual targets and evaluate their own progress towards them, supported participation in reviews.

Table 2.1 Continued

National policy: working in partnership with other agencies	Strategic implications for schools
Expectation of integrated local services – health/social services/education.	May choose to invest school SEN/inclusion funding in purchasing multi-agency services such as speech and language intervention, mental health services.
Expectation that schools will work closely and effectively with outside agencies.	Review organisational structures so that outside agencies have a clear point of contact; review time available for class teachers for liaison and joint planning with outside agencies.
National policy: inclusion	**Strategic implications for schools**
Schools are expected to review cultures, policies and practice to ensure that all children are included; schools are expected to identify and remove barriers to learning and participation.	May want to revise organisational structures so that SEN sits within a broader inclusion remit. Will need to review school cultures, policies and practice systematically, using a tool such as the CSIE *Index for Inclusion* (2002).
Children must be educated in mainstream schools unless that is incompatible with the wishes of the parent or the efficient education of other children.	Need to plan for staff training in meeting more complex SEN.
Special schools are expected to develop new roles, working closely with mainstream.	May want to investigate partnership with one or more special schools – sharing of expertise, shared teaching on mainstream site of groups of children on special school roll.
National policy: tackling disability discrimination	**Strategic implications for schools**
Schools must not, by law, treat disabled pupils less favourably than others, or discriminate against them in their admission arrangements or any of the services they offer.	Need to review all relevant school policies. Need to ensure all staff have had disability awareness training. Need to ensure policy and practice on bullying takes account of disability. Need to check when planning SEN provision that children are not excluded from school activities, e.g. offered a restricted curriculum, sent home at lunchtime because of behaviour problems in unstructured time. Ongoing training for staff in making the curriculum more accessible.
Schools must plan and keep under review a written accessibility strategy.	Need to plan regular review of accessibility strategy as part of the strategic management cycle (evaluation stage) and consider its implications for budgetary planning.
National policy: focus on outcomes, raising standards and doing what works	**Strategic implications for schools**
Increased emphasis on schools exploiting best practice when devising interventions.	Revise patterns of provision after seeking evidence on 'what works?' (see Chapter 7).

Table 2.1 Continued

National policy: focus on outcomes, raising standards and doing what works	Strategic implications for schools
LEAs and schools expected to define outcomes to be achieved through provision.	Expected outcomes set as targets within strategic management cycle.
Rates of progress to be measured as part of School Action and School Action Plus.	Need to put in place systems to find out if provision is enabling pupils to make progress.
National policy: reducing bureaucracy and teacher workload	**Strategic implications for schools**
Reduction in number of stages in revised SEN Code of Practice; shorter, simpler IEPs; IEPs only required for provision that is additional to and different from the normal differentiated curriculum; IEPs not required if child's needs can be addressed through regular curriculum planning.	Implement whole-school planning to meet diversity, so as to reduce the need for large numbers of IEPs (see Chapter 8).
National policy: importance of key transitions	**Strategic implications for schools**
Expectation of information exchange and careful joint planning when children move from Early Years setting to primary; from primary to secondary; and from school to further education, training or employment.	May need to plan for better transfer of information, induction, multi-agency forward planning.
National policy: new roles for SENCO	**Implications for schools**
Emphasis on role of SENCO in determining the strategic direction of SEN policy and provision, as well as the operational day-to-day role. Emphasis on SENCO's role in providing professional guidance to colleagues, including monitoring the quality of teaching standards and monitoring of pupils' achievements. Increased management role, with larger numbers of teaching assistants in the team.	Need to review role and examine implications for training and time allocation.

Taking stock of local priorities

As well as the national priorities outlined above, you will want to build local priorities into your strategic analysis of 'what's out there'. The LEA's Education Development Plan (EDP) or SEN and Inclusion Development Plan can be a useful source of information on key issues for LEA schools as a whole in relation to SEN, and on where the LEA is planning to target resources and energy to address the identified priorities. For example, the EDP might identify behaviour difficulties and a very high rate of exclusions from school as a key issue for the LEA, and set out the support and training which schools might expect to access over the period of the plan. It might set out a three- or five-year strategy in relation to the role of special schools. It might identify a large local increase in the numbers of pupils with autistic spectrum disorder, and set out a plan to develop provision in new resource bases in mainstream schools. It might offer opportunities for multi-agency projects, which schools can bid into.

These are all important issues which will have an impact on the strategic choices you make in your school development or improvement plan.

Pupil needs analysis

Another influence on your strategic choices will be an analysis of the likely future profile of SEN within the school. There are several steps involved here:

- rolling forward the current profile of numbers of children with each need type (communication and interaction, social, emotional and behavioural needs, sensory or physical impairment, cognition and learning). This allows you to see (at least for the next school year) where there will need to be particular patterns of provision – more provision for children with behaviour difficulties in next year's Year 5, for example, or a reduced need for in-class support for pupils with learning difficulties in Year 9; and
- taking account of local trends such as increases in the numbers of children on the autistic spectrum, or the numbers of children with moderate learning difficulties remaining in mainstream school with support, rather than moving to special provision.

Such trends and projections will inform planning for staff development as well as for provision.

Asking stakeholders what they want

The final element of this strategic analysis is some form of discussion with pupils, parents/carers, school staff and outside agencies about what they would see as priorities for the future. With staff and outside agencies this will be relatively easy: they are likely to have strong views on the support they need, as class and subject teachers, or – from the outside agencies' perspective – what the school is doing well and where there might be room for development. Parents/carers and pupils present a greater challenge, but one where:

- the local parent partnership organisation may have valuable feedback to give about any issues that have come up across their contacts with parents of children at the school;
- a parent governor may have gathered views;
- any regular meeting which the SENCO has with a group of parents can be opened up for discussion about future directions;
- the SENCO may be able to report on themes arising from what children say, in the course of reviews, about the support they receive; or

- circle time might have a one-week focus across the school on any difficulties which children have with their work or in 'social' times – what helps them and what more could be done.

STEP FOUR: setting targets for SEN and inclusion

After the evaluation phase in the strategic management cycle comes target-setting. Earlier in this chapter we looked at how broad policy objectives can lead to measurable targets. Examples were given of such targets, drawn from policy objectives about raising attainment and promoting inclusion.

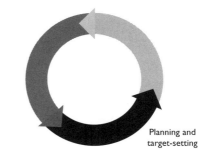

Planning and target-setting

Figure 2.5 The school improvement cycle

In this section we will look at further examples of targets, beginning with those for pupil attainment.

Targets for attainment

Targets for attainment can be set in relation to **absolute** attainment of a cohort of pupils at the end of their key stage, or in relation to their **progress** over a key stage.

There has long been an SEN myth that, outside of the QCA 'P' scales, there are no tools for measuring attainment which allow comparisons across schools. This ignores the fact that for some groups of pupils – those with sensory or physical impairment in the absence of learning difficulties, for example, or social, emotional and behavioural difficulties (SEBD) , or in some cases autistic spectrum disorder (ASD) – it is reasonable to expect that they will attain at least the national benchmark levels (level 2 at Key Stage 1, level 4 at Key Stage 2, level 5 at Key Stage 3). For these children it is important to check whether, in your school, they do attain at this level. It also ignores the fact that the majority of pupils with other types of SEN – difficulties in cognition and learning or speech and language – will attain national curriculum levels, albeit below the national benchmarks, at the end of their key stage. These lower NC levels can be used by schools to set whole-school targets, for example, for the percentage of an SAT cohort who will attain at least level 1 at the end of Key Stage 1, at least level 3 at the end of Key Stage 2, at least level 4 at the end of Key Stage 3 and at least one GCSE A*–C at the end of Key Stage 4.

Sometimes it is clearer and more meaningful to phrase these targets in terms of reducing the numbers of pupils who fail to achieve very basic literacy, mathematics and scientific skills – for example:

- to reduce the percentage of the 2004 cohort who reach the end of Key Stage 2 attaining below level 3 in English from a current 18% to 6%;

- to reduce the difference in the percentage who attain below level 3 in mathematics and those who attain below level 3 in English at the end of Key Stage 2 by 3%; or
- to reduce the percentage of pupils failing to attain even one GCSE from 6% to 4%.

Such targets allow a comparison of the percentage of very low attainers in the school, year on year, and, with due attention to particular cohort factors, can be a useful way of evaluating the effectiveness of the provision which the school is making for children who experience difficulties in the core subjects. They will also allow the school to compare their own performance with that of all schools across the country: national figures for the percentage of children below level 1 (Key Stage 1), below level 3 (Key Stage 2) and below level 4 (Key Stage 3) are published annually by the DfES in its *Statistics for Education*, available on the internet at www.dfes.gov.uk/statistics. It should also be possible, using LEA data, to make comparisons with other similar schools, i.e. those in the same group for prior attainment or for the percentage eligible for Free School Meals (FSM).

Such comparisons can be illuminating. In one LEA known to the authors, for example, some schools in the same FSM group would have no children below level 3 at the end of KS2 in English and mathematics, while others would have 40 per cent or more, despite having a lower percentage of EAL learners and children with high-funded, severe and complex SEN in the relevant cohort.

Value added data, which measures pupils' progress over a key stage, are increasingly available and even more useful than measures of 'absolute' attainment, since they take into account variations between schools in the make-up of their cohorts and the extent to which they operate inclusive policies. Schools need to be able to compare the progress made by children starting a key stage with above-average, average and below-average attainment with the progress made nationally, using data supplied by their LEA and the progress charts available in the DfES Autumn Package. Such comparisons will enable them to set targets like these:

- to increase the percentage of children in the school who start their key stage with below-average attainment, and by the end of the key stage have made progress at above the national average level;
- to decrease the percentage of children in the cohort who make less than one level jump (or equivalent points score gain) over the key stage;
- to increase the percentage of children with EBD who make points score progress (averaged across the three core subjects) above the national average level by the end of the key stage; or
- to reduce the percentage of boys with below-average attainment at the start of the key stage who make progress at less than the national average level by the end of the key stage.

Increasing use of the 'P' scales will add further refinements, as we become able to track progress from 'P' level starting points to other 'P' levels and to NC levels – from P4 at the start of Key Stage 1 to P8 at the end, for example, or from P8 at the start of Key Stage 2 to level 2 at the end of Key Stage 2 or level 3 at the end of Key Stage 3. Ultimately, national data of this kind will also be available, broken down into various types of SEN. These will enable schools to compare the progress made by, say, a child with ASD with national expectations for children with ASD and the same starting point (P level or NC level).

At the time of writing we are still some distance away from accessing data of this kind. Consultation is just beginning on the need types on which progress data should be gathered; much remains to be done on the moderation systems which will give schools confidence in 'P' level judgements, and on the systems (PANDAs and Autumn Package information) for providing schools and LEAs with comparative data.

For the moment, schools will need to start from what is available: the relatively crude figures on the percentages of very low attainers at the end of each key stage, and any local data their LEA is able to supply on pupil progress in relation to below-average starting points.

Targets for behaviour and social inclusion

Attainment targets link to one aspect of a school's SEN provision: that for children who experience difficulties in learning. Most schools, however, also make some kind of provision designed to reduce the incidence of social, emotional and behavioural difficulties, irrespective of whether or not these are associated with difficulties in learning.

Schools vary in the extent to which they are able to set targets for this element of their provision, or measure progress over time. Some (mainly secondary schools) will have in place elaborate systems for measuring various behavioural indicators across the school, along with associated targets for improvement. They might, for example, set targets to

- reduce the frequency with which pupils are sent out of lessons to 'time out'/withdrawal rooms across the school, or in specified year groups, or in specified curriculum subjects;
- reduce the percentage of the school population who are permanently excluded, or experience at least one fixed-term exclusion;
- reduce the number of days lost to fixed-term exclusion overall, or in specified year groups; or
- reduce the percentage of pupils who, after one fixed-term exclusion, go on to have further fixed-term exclusions.

Primary schools are often less accustomed to target-setting in this area. They tend to make less use of exclusions, and may thus not be able to compare their own performance with that of similar schools.

They do, however, often have internal indicators of the extent of behavioural difficulties in the school which will at least allow them to compare figures year on year within their own school, or across year groups: the percentage of the school population who have their name entered at least once in the head teacher's Behaviour Book, for example, or the percentage of the school population which has been excluded at least once from the school playground at lunchtime. It is important that you use whatever school systems are already in place to log behaviour, for the wider purpose of assessing each year whether things seem to be getting better or worse on the behaviour front and what therefore has been the impact of SEN/inclusion provision or other initiatives. The same measures can then be used to set improvement targets.

Some schools are also becoming experienced in using more positive, sophisticated measures of pupils' social, emotional and behavioural competence, either home-grown or developed from published rating scales and observational tools. Examples might be measures of emotional literacy (Morris 2002), and the QCA's target-setting rating scales for conduct behaviour, emotional behaviour and learning behaviour (QCA 2001). Use of scales like these might, for example, enable a school to set targets such as:

- there will be an average increase of two points on the QCA learning behaviour scale in Year 5, over the course of one school year;
- scores on the Emotional Intelligence Questionnaire for pupils identified as experiencing SEBD in our school will rise by at least 20 per cent by 2004.

Targets for inclusion

Targets for the inclusion of pupils with SEN might include, at the simplest level:

- to reduce the number of children living in the school's catchment area who attend special schools or units rather than your school;
- to reduce the percentage of the school population who leave to attend a special school or unit elsewhere, either during a key stage or, for example, at primary–secondary transfer;
- to increase the percentage who re-integrate from special school or unit placements elsewhere.

Numbers are likely to be small, however, and not always meaningful; they are about children's presence but not necessarily about their participation in the mainstream. We need to put time into developing some of the more subtle ways of measuring inclusion that we looked at earlier in this chapter – the extent of social integration with the peer group, for example, for children with complex SEN, the percentage of the school day in which they are taught with peers rather than in separate provision, their engaged time within the classroom, or their participation in extra-curricular activities.

Schools using the CSIE *Index for Inclusion* (Centre for Studies in Inclusive Education 2002) will also be able to use success criteria linked to the actions they have identified following self review as their inclusion targets.

Other kinds of targets

Many schools already include in their annual governors' report to parents statistics on the percentage of children moving 'down' from School Action Plus to School Action, or off School Action altogether. This is a useful measure of the effectiveness of SEN intervention, but not a target. To translate it into a target, the school would need to compare the percentages moving 'down' a stage year on year, and decide on a reasonable level of challenge: for example 'to increase the percentage of children with SEN who have moved down a stage over the course of one year from 10% to 15%'.

Much less useful are Code-related targets linked to the percentage of children achieving some or all of their IEP targets. There is an obvious circularity in the annual governors' report claiming proudly that a high percentage of children met the targets on their IEPs, when IEP targets are intended from the start to be inherently within the child's reach (**s**pecific, **m**easurable, **a**chievable, **r**ealistic and **t**ime-constrained). Schools which are skilled at setting SMART targets are likely to do well on this measure; those that are not will do less well – irrespective of the actual progress which children are making in learning or behaviour.

A final type of target, linked closely to strategic thinking, derives from the School Development or Improvement Plan. Such targets often appear as success criteria for particular actions in the Plan: if, for example, the school is planning to increase the involvement of pupils with SEN in the process of assessment and action planning to meet their needs, the SDP might list a number of actions accompanied by success criteria/targets such as these:

- 80 per cent of IEP planning meetings will have the pupil present for at least part of the time;
- 100 per cent of pupils will record their views on their own progress and next steps, with adult support where necessary, before the annual review of their Statement.

If the SDP has a set of actions designed to develop inclusive teaching skills across the school, there might be a target such as:

- 90 per cent of teachers' curriculum planning will show annotation for individuals or groups of pupils with additional needs, which specifies appropriate learning objectives, teaching styles and access strategies;
- at least five items from an inclusive teaching observation checklist are evident in 90 per cent of classroom observations conducted in the course of the year.

It is likely that targets like these will be a subset of a larger group covering inclusion in its wider sense – targets related to the attainment of looked-after pupils, for example, or to attendance and punctuality, or to reducing bullying in all its forms, or the attainment of gifted and talented pupils or those from different ethnic groups. Cheminais (2001) has a helpful list of such success criteria, showing 'value added' for schools which are working to remove barriers to learning for all their pupils, and particularly for those who may be at risk, for whatever reason.

Why set measurable targets?

Schools understandably feel weighed down by the statutory target-setting processes and the volume of the data which they are expected to gather, understand and use. In this climate the idea of setting targets for SEN may feel like a bridge too far.

Schools may also feel – SENCOs in particular – that as children with SEN are highly individual and demonstrate particularly idiosyncratic and erratic patterns of achievement, it is not meaningful to set whole-school targets for their progress. IEPs, they may feel, are sufficient, particularly when cohorts are small.

Another view is that it is inappropriate to use 'hard' targets (data on attainment or exclusions, for example) for pupils with SEN, because their progress needs to be measured differently – in terms of self-confidence, perhaps, or other intangibles that do not lend themselves to measurement.

All these arguments have some legitimacy. We could, if we accept them, go on as we have for the last 20 years – spending more and more money each year on provision for individual children, without ever stopping to ask tough questions about whether what we are doing is actually making a difference in terms of raising attainment and promoting inclusion for our most vulnerable pupils.

Alternatively, we could put in place systems – at school, LEA and national level – which do hold us to account for what we achieve with these children, just as we are held to account for what we achieve with those who are judged able to achieve national expectations.

Without such systems, schools will have difficulty, in a climate of increased delegation of funding along with an associated increase in responsibilities, in proving that they are doing a good job and spending their money wisely. More importantly, they are unlikely to be able to learn from their own successes and those of others, or to improve the services they offer. As Osborne and Gaebler (1992) put it:

> What gets measured gets done.
> If you don't measure results, you can't tell success from failure.
> If you can't see success, you can't reward it.
> If you can't reward success, you are probably rewarding failure.
> If you can't see success, you can't learn from it.
> If you can't recognise failure, you can't correct it.
> If you can demonstrate results, you can win support.

How to use targets wisely

Measurable targets are a starting point in improving what we do, but not the end point. If they are to be effective, there must be intermediate processes which translate broad school-level targets into the detail of what actually happens in classrooms and around the school.

Much of the opposition to measurement and target-setting arises from things that go wrong in these intermediate processes, not from the targets themselves. It has been well documented, for example, that some targets and the testing that goes with them can push teachers into a teaching style that emphasises 'transmission teaching of knowledge, thereby favouring those students who prefer to learn in this way and disadvantaging and lowering the self-esteem of those who prefer more active learning experiences' (Harlen and Deakin Crick 2002). Teaching to the test, over-concern with performance rather than process, reduced intrinsic motivation and increased extrinsic motivation have become all-too-familiar features of some classrooms since high-stakes testing and targets were introduced for pupils of average attainment and above.

At the same time, however, we have learned a great deal about how to use the performance climate productively, translating crude numerical targets into meaningful learning goals for individuals, and involving pupils actively in owning these goals, in understanding what they need to do to reach them, and taking some responsibility for assessing their own progress. Black *et al.* (2002) provide a blueprint for such formative assessment. Because of their motivational effects, models like these are even more essential for those who are experiencing difficulties in learning: without them, no amount of target-setting on its own will raise standards or help promote inclusion.

3 School self-evaluation

Introduction

In this chapter we will re-enter the strategic management cycle at the evaluation stage and look at a practical framework which schools can use to answer the questions:

- How well are we doing, in relation to our SEN policy objectives?
- How do we compare with similar schools?
- How well *should* we be doing?

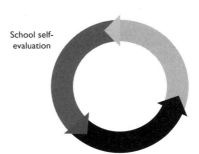

School self-evaluation

Figure 3.1 The school improvement cycle

The self-evaluation framework can be used in a number of ways:

- some parts will be done annually within the regular cycle of school development/improvement planning and reporting to parents on the implementation of the SEN policy: for example, evaluating the school's performance using quantitative data which allow for comparison with similar schools;
- other parts will be done only when the school wants to conduct an in-depth analysis of one or more aspects of its SEN and inclusion practice; or
- schools may want to use the whole framework to help them prepare for an Ofsted inspection.

The suggested framework links to the broader school self-evaluation methodology on which many senior managers have had local, Ofsted-accredited training.

Components of self-evaluation

Two kinds of self-evaluation	
Quantitative	**Qualitative**
Attainment data	Checklist of quality features
Behaviour data	Observing lessons
Inclusion data	Scrutinising IEPs and teachers' planning
SEN Code of Practice data	Talking with pupils and looking at their work
	Talking with other stakeholders

Quantitative methods focus on 'hard' evidence from National Curriculum assessment and other attainment measures, along with data on behaviour, inclusion and children's progress within the SEN Code's graduated approach to assessment and intervention.

Qualitative methods draw on 'softer' (but no less valid information) from classroom observation, looking at pupils' work, and talking with them and other stakeholders.

Quantitative self-evaluation

Quantitative self-evaluation uses measures similar to those which we looked at in Chapter 2 in relation to target-setting. In this chapter we will consider them in a little more detail, under the four headings of Attainment, Behaviour, Inclusion and SEN Code of Practice data.

Attainment
Below are examples of attainment data which you might analyse in your quantitative self-evaluation:

- The percentage of children attaining below level 1 in the core subjects in Key Stage 1 end of Key Stage assessment, below level 3 in Key Stage 2, below level 4 in Key Stage 3, and failing to attain at least one GCSE A* to C at Key Stage 4 – compared with the percentage in previous years, with the national percentage (available each year in the DfES *Statistics of Education Bulletin*) and with any available information on percentages in similar schools locally or nationally.
- The percentage of children in the cohort with SEN but without global learning difficulties who achieve the nationally expected levels at the end of their key stage, compared with the overall percentage achieving the nationally expected levels. This might include children with sensory or physical impairment, Asperger syndrome/ASD, SEBD or specific learning difficulties/dyslexia.

- The progress over a key stage made by children who come from a below-average starting point at the beginning of the key stage, compared with the same measure for previous school cohorts and the national average progress.
- Average gains on standardised tests of reading, spelling or mathematics made by children receiving additional help – for example, the average reading age change in months per year or the average change in standardised score on a maths test given at the beginning and end of the year.

The data which you analyse will depend to an extent on the data package which the LEA makes available to its schools, and national developments in the Autumn Package, and PANDAs as they emerge over the next few years.

Some schools, particularly those with large cohorts or high percentages of children with special educational needs, will also be in a position to make more sophisticated analyses, breaking down further the SEN data suggested above by gender, ethnicity and SEN need type.

CASE STUDY

This case study gives an example of the data assembled and analysed by one school – a medium-sized, all-through primary school in an area characterised by high social deprivation – with help from its LEA.

In Key Stage 1, the school found that far more children were failing to achieve at least Level 1 in reading, writing and maths than in similar schools within the LEA (Table 3.1). The head teacher and SENCO wondered if this might be because the school was more inclusive than others – that is, having a higher percentage of children with complex SEN on their roll, or a higher percentage of EAL learners. Data provided by the LEA (Table 3.2) showed that this was not so, however: other schools had higher percentages of children with complex SEN or EAL but fewer pupils below Level 1 – in some cases no pupils at this level.

By the end of Key Stage 2 the picture was very different. While the school still had more very low-attaining children (below Level 3) than the average for similar schools, the difference was very small – particularly for mathematics (Table 3.3).

Table 3.1 Data analysis – a case study. Percentage of children attaining below level 1 (codes D + W) at the end of Key Stage 1

	Percentage in our school (%)	LEA average for similar schools (%)	Overall LEA average (%)	National average (%)
Reading	30.3	11.0	3.9	3
Writing	33.3	17.4	5.6	4
Mathematics	24.2	7.6	2.5	2

Table 3.2 Comparison with similar schools in our LEA – that is schools with more than 50% of pupils eligible for Free School Meals – for Reading in Key Stage 1

	Number of pupils in cohort (%)	Percentage below level 1 (%)	Percentage of pupils in the school with English as an additional language (%)	Percentage of pupils in the cohort with complex SEN (i.e. individual allocations of more than £3,000) (%)
Our school	54	30.3	37	3.7
School A	22	0	51.4	0
School B	44	13.6	0	4.5
School C	39	12.8	0	0
School D	31	19.3	63.8	0
School E	20	5	28	0
School F	12	0	2.5	0
School G	37	10.81	1.1	0
School H	23	13.0	7.5	0
School I	25	0	3.8	4
School J	21	14.3	2.3	0.
School K	35	8.6	1.3	2.9
School L	54	3.7	25.3	9.3
School M	20	15.0	2.9	5.0
School N	19	10.5	0	5.3

Table 3.3 Percentage of children attaining below level 3 (codes D + B + N + 2) at the end of Key Stage 2

	Percentage in our school (%)	LEA average for similar schools (%)	Overall LEA average (%)	National average (%)
English	22.2	18.9	7.8	7
Mathematics	17.8	16.8	7.2	5

Something, it seemed was happening in Key Stage 2 to help more children achieve basic skills – but not in Key Stage 1. Analysis of value added data (Figure 3.2) confirmed this picture. Progress of children beginning Key Stage 2 with below-average attainment (average points score below 15) was generally above the national average – again, especially in maths.

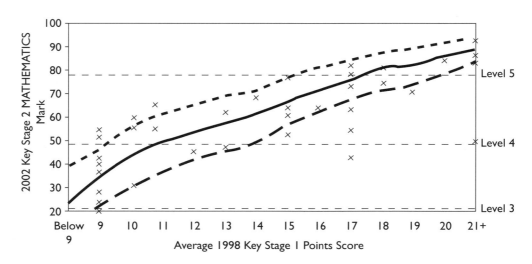

Source: DfES Autumn Package. The solid line (the median) shows the Key Stage 2 result achieved by a pupil in the middle of the national distribution. The upper (dotted) line shows the Key Stage 2 result achieved by a pupil three-quarters of the way up the national distribution (upper quartile). The lower (dashed) line shows the result achieved by a pupil a quarter of the way up (lower quartile). The crosses show the results achieved by the pupils in the case study school.

Figure 3.2   Progress between Key Stages 1 and 2: value added data for our school, showing progress over the Key Stage made by children starting Key Stage 2 in 1998

The Level 4+ attainment of children with SEN but without global learning difficulties (Table 3.4) was good in mathematics – nearly up to the average for the school as a whole. In English it was not so good: in part, predictably, due to the number of children with dyslexic difficulties in the cohort, and the difficulty a child with autistic spectrum disorder had in understanding fiction and writing imaginatively. The data still raised questions, however, about why only one of the four children with SEBD had attained Level 4+.

The newly introduced, structured one-to-one literacy programme in Key Stage 2 was proving very effective (Table 3.5). Children on the programme were making progress at approximately twice the average rate for all children, over the six-month period of the intervention. The school decided, however, that it would also want evidence on whether these rapid gains were maintained over time, and

Table 3.4   Percentage of children with SEN but without global learning difficulties who attained at or above the nationally expected levels

In Key Stage 1 there were only two children in this category; one child attained a level 2 and one child a level W – but the numbers involved are too small for meaningful analysis.

In Key Stage 2, nine children out of the cohort of 54 had identified needs of this type – one child with ASD, one child with a visual impairment, four children with social, emotional and behavioural needs and three children with dyslexic difficulties. Of these children, 33% achieved level 4+ in English compared to 65% of the school cohort as a whole, and 67% in maths compared to 70% in the cohort as a whole.

Table 3.5   Average gain on standardised tests

This year the school assessed children for reading accuracy and comprehension on the Individual Reading Analysis (published by NFER-Nelson) before and after they completed a new, structured 1–1 literacy programme in Key Stage 2. They made an average gain of 13 months in accuracy and 11 months in comprehension, over a six-month period.

planned to retest the group annually on the same reading test and to track their progress through to their end-of-key stage tests.

Overall, the head and SENCO reached the conclusion that the school's SEN provision in Key Stage 2 was successful in raising attainment, when compared to similar schools in the LEA. More children still left the school in Year 6, however, with very low literacy and mathematical skills than the national average, so there was still much work to be done to improve outcomes further. The newly introduced literacy intervention looked promising, but its impact would need to be followed up over a period of time.

In Key Stage 1, the school concluded that there was much room for improvement. They decided to find out how the schools in the area with better Key Stage 1 outcomes organised their provision for children with SEN. Comparing provision maps (see Chapter 6), they found that other schools were investing far more than they were in Key Stage 1 provision: usually this was funded from the school's own additional educational needs budget. The case study school, however, spent most of its additional educational needs budget on reducing class sizes slightly across the school. Its SEN provision was largely funded by the LEA, with School Action Plus money attached to individual pupils entering Key Stage 2 with low prior attainment, and through Statements. They were surprised to find that their spending patterns were so different from those in similar schools, and resolved to review them.

From the data on the end-of-key stage attainment of pupils with SEN but without global learning difficulties, the school concluded that it might need to raise its expectations of what pupils could be expected to achieve in literacy – particularly those with SEBD. They decided to do more work with individual children and their parents/carers in future, setting challenging targets and working with the children on the things they would need to be able to know, understand and do in order to achieve them.

Behaviour

These are some examples of the behaviour data which you might analyse in your quantitative school self-evaluation:

- the exclusion rate (percentage of the school roll who experience permanent exclusion, or number of permanent exclusions per 1,000 pupils, compared to LEA and national averages);
- the percentage of pupils permanently excluded from the school with identified SEN compared with the percentage of the total school

population who have SEN (for example, pupils with SEN made up 55 per cent of those permanently excluded from school but only 25 per cent of the school population) compared to any local data which may be available;

- the percentage of the school roll who experienced at least one fixed-term exclusion, compared to LEA and national averages;
- the percentage of pupils with identified SEN who experienced at least one fixed-term exclusion, compared with the percentage of the total school population who have SEN (for example, pupils with SEN made up 40 per cent of those experiencing at least one fixed-term exclusion but only 25 per cent of the school population);
- the total number of school days lost to fixed-term exclusions over the school year, compared to LEA and national averages;
- the percentage of pupils who, after one fixed-term exclusion, go on to have one or more further fixed-term exclusions, compared with the school percentage for previous years, and with any available local data;
- the number of referrals to withdrawal rooms/time out rooms/head teacher or senior manager's office, compared with the school's figure for previous years, and broken down, where appropriate, by year group and/or curriculum/subject area.

Other behaviour data collected in school, for example:

- information from commercially available behaviour databases;
- playground exclusions;
- names in school behaviour books;
- pupil ratings on measures of social competence, self-esteem, behaviour.

Again, the precise data which you gather on behaviour will be influenced by local practice: wherever possible you will want to use measures which are not unique to your own situation, but which allow you to compare your school with others.

CASE STUDY

The case study school whose attainment data we considered earlier in this chapter collected the following data on behaviour:

- The school had never, neither this year nor previously, permanently excluded a pupil: in this they differed from others in the LEA where the overall primary exclusion rate was one child per 1,000.
- They also made almost no use of fixed-term exclusions, preferring instead to use internal exclusion, where the child would work on his/her own outside the head teacher's office for a day or more. No data were gathered, however, on the numbers of such internal exclusions, whether children with SEN were more or less likely to experience an internal exclusion than other children, or

whether the internal exclusions were effective in helping children to make changes to their behaviour – that is, what percentage of children who had one such internal exclusion then went on to have others.

- Some children were also informally excluded at lunchtimes, with their parents/carers being asked to pick them up and keep them at home over the lunch period if they had persistently been in trouble in the playground. These informal arrangements were not documented, however, so the school had no way of knowing whether its new lunchtime policy of organised playground games, or its new Peer Mediation scheme, were having an impact.

The school concluded that they were probably successful in the provision they made for individual children with SEBD, and their wider work on behaviour and emotional literacy across the schools (regular circle times in every classroom, for example), but that they would need to set up some simple systems for gathering better data in the future, in order to be sure.

Inclusion

Data on the inclusion of pupils with SEN or disabilities which you might analyse could include:

- numbers of children with postcodes for your catchment area who attend special schools or units;
- numbers of children leaving the school for special schools, compared year on year;
- numbers reintegrated to the school from special school placements; and
- data from systematic observation of the extent to which pupils with complex SEN are socially integrated within the peer group, are taught within regular classes rather than in separate provision, can access the full curriculum and take part in extra-curricular activities (see Chapter 2).

CASE STUDY

Our case study school asked the LEA to print from its database of children in special schools and units a list of children with postcodes showing that they lived in the school's catchment area. The list showed that one child attended a special school for children with severe learning difficulties, two attended the local school for children with moderate learning difficulties and one a special school for deaf children. The SENCO volunteered to make contact with these schools, meet the children and explore possibilities for making links.

The school very rarely had children leaving for special school placements during their primary years, although, each year, one or two Year 6 pupils did go on to special school placement (moderate learning difficulties or SEBD) at key stage transfer. No children had reintegrated from the local moderate learning difficulties special school, with which the school had very little contact. On the other hand, the school noted that it had this year successfully reintegrated two children who had been permanently excluded from other local primary schools.

Informally, they felt that children with complex SEN in the school were socially well integrated, with the predictable exception of their two autistic pupils. No systematic information had ever been collected, however, to test this out, or to look at curriculum access in the classroom.

The school concluded that their analysis gave further evidence of their strength in meeting the needs of children with social, emotional and behavioural difficulties, and of an inclusive culture where belief systems emphasised meeting the needs of all pupils from the local community. They decided, however, that they needed to probe more deeply to see how this culture was translated into practice, and the extent to which children were included in friendship groups and appropriately differentiated classroom teaching. They also decided to do more work next year with Year 5 pupils who had complex SEN, to prepare them for secondary school transfer and to liaise well ahead of time with local secondary schools. They felt this would increase the chances of the children remaining in the mainstream once they left the primary school.

SEN Code of Practice data

As we saw in Chapter 2, there is useful information to be gained from recording, year on year, the percentage of children moving between the levels of graduated response to SEN set out in the Code of Practice. You might want to analyse the percentage of children moving:

- from School Action to School Action Plus;
- from School Action Plus to a Statement;
- from a Statement to School Action Plus, School Action, or normal differentiated curriculum;
- from School Action Plus to School Action or normal differentiated curriculum; and
- from School Action to a normal differentiated curriculum.

In each case you would need to compare these figures with the figures for previous years and any available data from local schools.

It can also be illuminating to examine, each year, the overall profile of numbers at each level. An expected profile can look something like this:

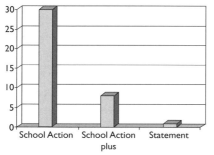

Figure 3.3 Code of Practice profile

The largest proportion of children with SEN is on School Action. For most of them School Action is successful in securing sufficient progress, so that a smaller percentage go on to School Action Plus – and an even smaller percentage (the extent varying according to LEA policies on Statementing) to a Statement.

CASE STUDY

Our case study school analysed its Code of Practice profile, which looked like this:

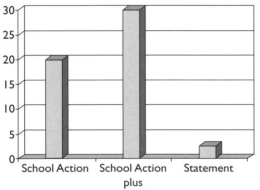

Figure 3.4 Code of Practice profile

The profile reflected the school pattern of relatively little provision for SEN in Key Stage 1, but a lot of provision in Key Stage 2 – funded by the LEA at School Action Plus as a consequence of high numbers of children leaving Key Stage 1 with very low attainment. It confirmed, for the school and the LEA, the need to look again at the school's provision map and consider retargeting some school funding for increased provision at School Action.

Qualitative self-evaluation

The examples and case study above showed what schools can learn from quantitative self-evaluation, particularly where it enables them to compare themselves with other schools, take steps to learn from those who are achieving more with their pupils, or to offer to share their good practice with others who are achieving less.

The examples also showed, however, that data alone rarely tell the whole story. Our case study school could only interpret its very different pattern of attainment across Key Stages 1 and 2 in the light of its knowledge about patterns of provision for SEN in the school. Their behaviour data of low permanent and fixed-term exclusions could be misleading, if it concealed a growing rate of lengthy internal exclusions or informal 'go home at lunch time' arrangements. Their data on inclusion told them whether pupils with complex

SEN were being locationally integrated – that is, educated on the same site as their peers. It did not tell them whether children were fully included, in the sense of inclusion into friendship groups, and full access to a curriculum which was specifically adapted to meet their needs.

Meaningful self-evaluation, then, has to go beyond the analysis of data and to look at the actual experience of pupils in your school.

In this section we will consider a range of tools which can be used by head teachers, SENCOs and other relevant senior managers to undertake this kind of qualitative evaluation.

Checklists

A good start to your school SEN self-evaluation is to complete a brief checklist of the key features of good practice in SEN and inclusion, as defined in the Ofsted framework. An example is given in Table 3.6.

Observing Lessons

Many school managers have had access in recent years to excellent training on how to observe lessons, in order to make judgements about the overall quality of teaching and learning, about classroom management, and about pupils' achievements and progress. Many schools, too, have developed policies which ensure that such observations are used positively, to identify strengths as well as areas for development, and to encourage mutual lesson observation by peers in a climate where staff support one another's learning.

Schools with a climate of this kind are also likely to allocate time to subject coordinator and SENCO to undertake classroom observation, so that it does not only rest with the head teacher or deputy but is part of a team approach.

It is very important that SENCOs do have this role, and the time to undertake it properly. Without classroom observation, they will not be able to bring their expertise to bear on the school improvement cycle at either the stage of school self-evaluation, or the stage of monitoring and evaluation.

The use of classroom observation for monitoring and evaluation is described in Chapter 4. This should be an ongoing process with a regular pattern of observations built into the SENCO's annual calendar.

For the purposes of school self-evaluation, the observations will take place over a shorter period and have a particular focus. The focus might arise from the school's analysis of its quantitative data, if this throws up patterns or hypotheses that need to be explored further. For example, the head teacher and SENCO might decide to look at the use of inclusive teaching strategies in classrooms across the school, using a checklist such as that provided by the National Literacy and Numeracy Strategies in their publication *Including All Children in the Literacy Hour and Daily Mathematics Lesson: A management guide* (DfES, 2002c).

Table 3.6 Qualitative indicators: school self-audit

School self-audit (adapted from Ofsted framework)	Fully	Partly	Not

➢ Do we have regard to the Code of Practice when meeting pupils' SEN?
  • We have an SEN policy that conforms to the requirements of the Code.
  • We have clear procedures for identifying pupils with SEN.
  • IEPs have SMART targets and pupil/parental involvement.
  • We follow the required procedures for annual and transition reviews.			

➢ Do we make our SEN Policy known to parents?
  • Material in prospectus;
  • Available in leaflet form;
  • Reported on annually to parents.			

➢ Do we make the provision on pupils' Statements? • A small sample of Statements link clearly to IEPs and classroom provision/practice.			
➢ Do we have a systematic process to improve teaching of pupils with SEN by observing lessons and providing feedback to teachers?			
➢ Do we regularly review our curriculum to ensure it matches the SEN of our pupils?			
➢ Do we analyse our assessment data to see if pupils with SEN are making good progress?			
➢ Does the governing body monitor the progress of pupils with SEN?			
➢ Are our admissions procedures inclusive?			
➢ Have we checked to see if pupils with SEN are treated unfairly or are experiencing bullying?			
➢ Are all pupils accessing a broad and balanced curriculum?			

Alternatively, the focus might be:

• the extent of links between children's Statements or IEPs and classroom or subject teaching;
• the effectiveness of the role of additional adults in supporting pupils with SEN;
• the effectiveness of classroom management of pupils with SEBD; or
• the extent to which pupils with SEN are developing independence.

Table 3.7 shows a proforma for planning classroom observation.

There is space on the proforma for head teachers or SENCOs to list the questions they will be asking as they make their observations. These need to be chosen to fit the identified focus for the observation, and might include a

Table 3.7 Planning classroom observations

Focus (Choose one from the list below)	Questions to ask myself in the observation
Use of inclusive teaching strategies	
Links between IEPs and classroom/subject teaching	
Effectiveness of additional adults in supporting pupils' learning	
Extent to which pupils are developing independence	
Effectiveness of classroom management for pupils with social, emotional and behavioural difficulties	
Other	

Plan for classroom observations

Where	When	By whom

selection of those from the Ofsted Framework and Ofsted guidance on Evaluating Educational Inclusion:

- Do teachers assess pupils' work thoroughly and use assessment to help and encourage pupils to overcome difficulties? For example, are they clear about what they want pupils with SEN to learn in the lesson, and what they have actually learnt? Do they show knowledge of pupils' learning targets by the way tasks are adapted and modified to match the objectives of the lesson?
- Do teachers use methods which enable all pupils to learn effectively? For example, do they use visual, kinaesethic and auditory learning pathways, interactive teaching styles, appropriate vocabulary, differentiated questioning?
- Do teachers manage pupils well and insist on high standards of behaviour?
- Do teachers use time, support staff and other resources, especially ICT, effectively?
- Does teaching help pupils to challenge stereotypes and appreciate diversity?

Scrutinising IEPs

Evaluating IEPs

- Are there meaningful objectives? Are these translated into SMART targets (success criteria for the objectives)?
- Do they have a small number of targets (three to four), related to key areas in communication, literacy, mathematics and aspects of behaviour or physical skills?
- Are the strategies for implementation clear, including who will do what and when?
- Do they describe access arrangements such as seating arrangements, teachers' use of language, use of visual and memory aids, buddying, grouping, pre-tutoring, signing, alternatives to pencil and paper tasks, scaffolding, use of appropriate ICT?
- Is there evidence of pupil and parental involvement?
- Do they help pupils to monitor their own progress?
- Are they impacting on teaching and learning?

Much has been made of scrutinising IEPs, and most SENCOs have had considerable training in this aspect of their work; we shall not spend much time on it here. The box above summarises the questions to be asked. The last question, 'Are IEPs impacting on teaching and learning?', is the most important. To assess this, it will be necessary to track beyond the IEP to the class or subject teacher's planning and then still further into lesson observation and looking at children's work.

Table 3.8 School self-evaluation: curriculum planning

	Yes	No	Partly
Is there any sign of differentiation for groups of pupils, or individuals, in the planning?			
If so, does it go beyond differentiation by outcome/adult support, so as to provide varied tasks for learners?			
Does it show learning objectives appropriate to different groups or individuals within the class – 'tracked back' within the same overall class topic for pupils with difficulties, 'tracked forward' for more able pupils?			
Does the teacher plan pupil groupings for specific purposes, or are pupils in fixed groupings no matter what the task?			
Are the roles of additional adults clearly specified?			
Are plans for units of work annotated to show particular access strategies/teaching styles matched to the needs of individuals in the class?			
Is there variety in the way pupils will record their work – in particular, planning for alternatives to paper-and-pencil tasks?			
Have plans been produced collaboratively, by year group or subject teams working with relevant specialists such as the SENCO or EAL coordinator?			

Scrutinising teachers' curriculum planning

Acres of carefully differentiated planning are not the be-all and end-all of effective classroom practice for children with SEN. The most inclusive teachers are often so fluent in the use of appropriate teaching styles and access strategies that they have little need to unpack them in written plans. Nevertheless, what teachers write on plans can give valuable insight into the impact of staff development work on differentiation.

Table 3.8 suggests some questions that a head teacher, SENCO or curriculum leader (ideally a SENCO and curriculum leader working together) might ask when looking at their colleagues' planning. The questions apply to planning for a wide range of needs, beyond SEN: more able pupils, for example, or EAL learners. They are about planning for inclusion in general, since there is a high degree of commonality in the features of good planning for all groups of pupils who may be regarded as vulnerable.

A key feature, which many teachers find difficult, is moving beyond differentiation 'by outcome', or 'by additional adult support', in their planning. Consider the examples below, drawn from medium-term literacy planning in one primary school:

Writing instructions		
Must (Red Group) Write simple instructions; may use personal register (you).	**Should (Blue Group)** Write instructions showing awareness of appropriate register, i.e. direct, impersonal. Use numbers to indicate sequence.	**Could (Green Group)** In addition to use of appropriate register, use organisational devices, e.g. arrows, lines, keys and boxes.

In this example the teacher planned for differentiation mainly in the sense of expecting less from a particular group. The task was not modified in any way.

Compare this with another example:

Red Group Sequence and label a series of diagrams that explain a process.	**Blue Group** Produce simple flowcharts or diagrams that explain the process.	**Green Group** Use own choice of organisational devices to present the text.

Here, the task has been modified to provide additional support for some pupils. Instead of producing diagrams from scratch they are given a series of pre-prepared diagrams to put in order and then label. With this support, they will be able to engage in the same learning about the features of instructional texts as any other group.

Here is another example:

Red Group As for Blue Group – teaching assistant works with the group to support.	**Blue Group** To produce a balanced report for a class newspaper using ICT.	**Green Group** Produce a report in the style of a newspaper studied.

In this example the differentiation is by additional adult support for a task which, again, has not otherwise been adapted. Contrast the example with the one below, where access strategies have been used to enable pupils to work independently.

Red Group Using layout devised in guided session, complete report in an electronic frame using on-screen word grids as support.	**Blue Group** Publish a newspaper style report electronically.	**Green Group** Edit stories to fit a particular space.

A second key issue to look for in planning is the extent to which pupil groupings are varied to match the different capabilities that pupils will bring to different tasks, and to provide opportunities for collaborative learning and peer support. Plans that have the red group, blue group and green group always working in these fixed groupings, no matter what the task (or sometimes, in the primary school, subject) are unlikely to be taking account of pupils' varying strengths and weaknesses. They are less likely to promote self-esteem and learning than plans which show pupils sometimes working independently in mixed-ability pairs or groups, sometimes in a group with others who are working on similar objectives (when the teacher plans to undertake some direct teaching) and sometimes on their own.

Plans should be clear about the role of any additional adults working with the teacher; one of the main purposes of writing down teaching plans is as a shared reference point for the teaching 'team', ensuring communication about who will do what, and when.

Where inclusive provision for pupils is good, plans will also demonstrate the use of additional adult support for pre-tutoring (individually or in groups), the use of a variety of media (visual, auditory and kinaesthetic) to present information, and use of the means of recording in addition to paper and pencil tasks. Gross (2002) provides a model of what such high-quality differentiated teacher planning will include; the National Literacy and Numeracy Strategies (DfES 2002c) have also published examples of how plans for units of work can be annotated in simple and straightforward ways to take account of the learning objectives, access strategies and teaching styles appropriate to individual learners in the class.

Looking at children's work

Looking at pupils' work is another essential tool in school self-evaluation. It will be most helpful when it has a well-delineated purpose – such as the work of pupils with a particular type of SEN, or in a particular curriculum area.

A joint work scrutiny by a curriculum coordinator and the SENCO may be particularly useful. Things to look out for include:

Progress of individuals
- Look at work of different dates.
- Is there evidence of progress?
- Is there a good variety of opportunities?
- Is there a good range of strategies to support recording, e.g. writing frames, ICT?

Comparing pupils in different year groups
- Is there progression as pupils get older?
- Is there evidence of a wide range of strategies to teach concepts as pupils get older?
- Are the resources age-appropriate?

Assessment and marking
- Are books marked well?
- Do pupils know what they need to do to improve?
- Is presentation consistent?
- Is work kept in an orderly way so progress can be reviewed?

Talking with pupils, parents and other stakeholders
Children themselves are often the best source of accurate information on whether the school's efforts to meet SEN are effective. They are able to add that essential extra dimension of what it *feels* like to have had their special educational needs identified, to have additional support, to take part in assessment, planning and review and to be taught in particular styles.

In Chapter 2 we looked at some ideas for gathering the pupil perspective, including summarising themes from pupils' contributions to IEP and Statement reviews, and the use of circle time. It may also be useful to engage a small number of pupils with SEN in a group discussion, using starting points such as:

- Can you tell me about things you enjoy and look forward to in school?
- Can you tell me about things you don't look forward to?
- In your classroom, who do you usually sit and work with – and how do you feel about that?
- How do you feel about...... (describe here any extra support provided)?
- Does any group of pupils have a hard time in this school? What sort of things happen? Do you think things get dealt with fairly?
- How about bullying – what do you think about that?
- Do you think you are doing as well as you can?
- What might help you do better?
- What would you really like to achieve in this school?
- Are there any things you think we should change about the way the school gives extra help to those who need it?

Shadowing one or more pupils with SEN over the course of a day, though time-consuming, can be a useful source of information about the impact of the school's SEN policies in practice, particularly in secondary schools.

The perspective of parents/carers of children with SEN also needs to be sampled as part of school self-evaluation. In Chapter 2 we considered the potential role of parent governors, the local parent partnership service or a termly meeting between the SENCO and a group of parents, in gathering this perspective. Key questions to investigate might be:

- What's going well – what has helped in meeting your child's SEN?
- What has not gone so well – and how might we have done things differently?
- How have you felt about the way in which we have discussed your child's difficulties with you?

- How have you felt about meetings you have attended?
- Have you felt involved in assessment and planning to meet your child's needs?

Finally, it is well worth asking outside agencies with whom the school regularly works to provide feedback on their perceptions about the school's strengths and areas for development in meeting SEN and the broader aspects of inclusion. Commenting 'cold' can be hard for external agencies, however, if a relationship of trust has not had time to develop. It may work best to involve them as a member of a review group, helping you plan the methods and tools you will use for your self-evaluation, and contributing in an ongoing way to the process of building up the picture of strengths and weaknesses which will form the basis of your school development planning.

4 Implementing and monitoring plans and provision

School development plans

Having now considered the process of self-evaluation and setting measurable targets within school development plans, we turn in this chapter to the implementation stage of the school improvement cycle, and to the place of monitoring in ensuring that progress is being made towards achieving those targets.

Every school has its preferred format for school development or

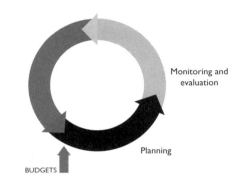

Figure 4.1 The school improvement cycle

improvement planning; it is not the intention here to go into detail on either formats or processes. All are likely to have in common the following:

- they will include measurable targets expressed as outcomes for pupils;
- they will describe the strategies and actions which will be put in place to meet the target;
- they will allocate resources (in time or money) to each of the strategies or actions;
- they will describe interim measures or milestones which will be evident if the planned strategies and actions are successfully beginning to have the required impact;
- they will describe the mechanisms which will be in place to gather information on the interim measures or milestones: who will do what to monitor progress on the plan, and when.

The strategies or actions taken to achieve the targets may involve implementing new forms of **provision** – for example, a lunchtime club to prevent behaviour difficulties, or a new reading programme. In Chapters 6 and 7 we will look at how schools can plan provision like this which will make a difference to the outcomes for children with SEN.

Other school development plan strategies will not be about provision, but about specific actions that staff will take to tackle a particular issue, such as increasing pupil or parental involvement, or increasing their skills in inclusive teaching.

Table 4.1 shows an extract from a school development plan (SDP) which illustrates both types of strategy: implementing new provision, and planning actions for key staff.

Monitoring plans and provision

Monitoring the impact of planned provision or action is fundamental to improving outcomes for children with SEN. It is also often the most neglected phase in the school improvement cycle: partly because monitoring feels intrinsically less interesting than making plans and carrying them out, and partly because of an undue degree of optimism in our belief that we can trust ourselves and others to carry out the actions we have planned, and that those actions will have the desired effect.

Monitoring in relation to SEN has two distinct elements:

- monitoring the implementation of the school development or improvement plan – to make sure that agreed actions are on track and that progress is being made towards achieving targets; and
- monitoring the quality, impact and value for money of ongoing SEN provision.

Both of these elements need a team approach, involving not only the SENCO but also curriculum coordinators and senior staff who can, as part of an overall monitoring brief, look at provision for children with SEN.

Monitoring the implementation of the SDP

Monitoring is most likely to happen if it is built in from the start to the school development or improvement plan itself. The plan in Table 4.1 is a good example of this: it describes in some detail the interim milestones which, if achieved, will demonstrate that the school is on track to achieve the targets in the plan. It also specifies who will check on progress in achieving the milestones.

Much SDP monitoring activity in schools tends to focus on whether the actions set out in the plan have been taken at the appropriate time. While this is necessary, it is not sufficient. Consider, for example, a plan to increase parental involvement by ringing parents regularly to encourage them to attend IEP and annual reviews. The SENCO might check files and find that colleagues were making the phone calls as planned, and believe that all is well. At the end of the year, however, it might become apparent that the percentage of parents attending reviews has not risen – perhaps because meetings were still being held at times which many parents could not make, or because the tenor of the phone calls was firm but not welcoming. Monitoring for early evidence of

Table 4.1   Extract from secondary school development plan

Long-term objective	Target	Action – who	Action – what	Action – when	Resources needed	Monitoring	Milestones
To raise the attainment of pupils with SEN: priority – literacy	At the end of KS3 all children will have a spelling age of at least 8 years. At the end of KS4 all children will have a spelling age of at least 9 years	NP	Network *Wordshark* (15 stations)	June 03	£400	Group spelling test twice a year	Learning support staff 100 per cent confident in using software by September
			Train learning support department in use of software	July 03			Average gains of at least 12 months in spelling age after 6 months
			Use weekly with bottom set English groups in Y7, 8, 9	Sept 03			
To promote inclusion: priority – behaviour	Fixed-term exclusions to reduce by 5 per cent	BR	Implement anger management groups in Y9	April 03	Buy-back from LEA behaviour support service £2,000	Review exclusion data from Leeds behaviour database half-termly	At least one group run by July 03
	Fixed-term exclusions of pupils receiving additional support to reduce by 10 per cent		Implement effective Pastoral Support Plans using activities/rewards linked to targets plus part-time college placements (KS4)	Sep 04	Canoeing/climbing/bowling vouchers £400 College placements £9,000		At least 10 college placements agreed for September Reduction in fixed-term exclusions each half-term
To raise the attainment of pupils with SEN: priority – parental involvement	95 per cent attendance by parents/carers at annual reviews; 75 per cent at IEP reviews	NP	Rewrite parents leaflet and SEN letters so that readability level is <9 years	June 03	£300 printing costs	Staff to record in register whether parents attended reviews; SENCO to monitor attendance termly	Termly monitoring shows increase in parental attendance at reviews
		Key workers and Heads of Year, supported by NP/BR	Set up frequent links with home from Y7 onwards through phone calls, positive letters home at least once a term, and home visits where necessary	Sept 03			File checks show positive letters home sent as per plan; 80 per cent response to parents' concerns within 48 hours by Dec. 03
	Response to parental concern within 48 hours	Learning mentors supported by NP	Research and compile a directory of contacts for parents: voluntary organisations/agencies/websites	June 03		Details of all communications with parents/carers to be recorded in SEN files, and dated. SENCO to monitor speed of response to parental concerns half-termly	

impact (in this case, checks at least termly on parents' attendance at reviews), as distinct from monitoring for evidence of **activity**, helps you to know whether the actions you have chosen for the SDP are the right actions – the ones that will make a difference. If they are not, monitoring allows plans to be adjusted rapidly.

Monitoring the quality and impact of ongoing SEN provision

Monitoring the provision your school makes for SEN involves both knowing what is happening for children within regular classroom teaching (the SEN Code's 'usual differentiated curriculum') and knowing about the quality and impact of additional provision (at School Action, School Action Plus or through Statements).

With any monitoring, all involved need to be clear about what is being monitored, and all monitoring should promote attention on positive outcomes for children which raise achievement. As such, monitoring may focus on:

- the quality of planning – realistic yet challenging individual and group targets, strategies which promote learning and engage interest, good use of resources both physical and human;
- the quality of teaching – clarity of learning objectives, engagement of children, knowledge of subject, ability to review or move learning on in response to child's understanding; and
- the quality of learning – interest shown by children, engagement in the activities, children's ability to generalise their learning, the speed at which they build on prior learning, the impact on their social and emotional wellbeing.

It is important that the whole process of monitoring and evaluating provision at whole-school level is made manageable. It is not possible to sit in on every lesson and every group session, or eavesdrop on every planned 1–1 interaction. Instead, you need to gain a snapshot of what the school is offering, to get a flavour of what it is like to plan for, deliver and receive within a SEN curriculum.

The tools for monitoring provision are those we have already looked at in Chapter 3: observing lessons, scrutinising planning and children's work and talking with pupils, parents and other stakeholders.

A process for using these tools needs to be mapped out so as to ensure coverage, over the year, of the different levels of provision (normal differentiated curriculum, additional provision at School Action and beyond) and of different year groups.

Table 4.2 shows an example of a monitoring schedule which one SENCO (also the Deputy Head) drew up to help her manage to best effect the limited time she had allocated for her monitoring role in a large primary school.

Her plan includes a note on the type of feedback which will be given to the staff involved: sometimes verbal only, sometimes followed up in writing – but always based on clear and pre-agreed criteria for what constitutes quality in

Table 4.2 SEN Monitoring Schedule 2002–2003

Ongoing Monitoring:
Weekly/termly data capturing (attendance, behaviour, attainment testing); weekly SENCO surgery Thursday 3.30–4.00

WHEN	WHAT	HOW	FEEDBACK
Autumn 1	Staff decisions on children to be involved in NLS, NNS catch-up programmes and literacy/maths School Action SEN intervention programmes	Overview of assessment results Involvement in prioritising needs	Direct discussion with staff/parents involved.
	Delivery of catch-up and intervention programmes	Sit in on selection of lessons with clear focus for monitoring	Verbal and written feedback using monitoring sheet
Autumn 2	Planning; IEP writing and monitoring of progress, differentiated curriculum planning	SENCO has time with each teacher to look at pupil needs, curriculum planning, IEPs	1–1 discussion, written feedback using monitoring sheet and where required follow up meeting
Spring 1	Progress of pupils on catch-up and intervention programmes	Overview of data leading to analysis Overview of selected pupil books	Feedback to staff involved and appropriate coordinators both informal and using monitoring sheets
Spring 2	Use of inclusive teaching strategies within lessons	Sit in on a selection of lessons with clear focus for monitoring	1–1 discussion using NLNS inclusive teaching observation checklist
Summer 1	Work scrutiny	Selection of books – children at SA and SA+ both literacy and maths against low/mid ability child	Informal verbal and written feedback using monitoring sheets
	Delivery of catch-up and intervention programmes	Sit in on selection of lessons with clear focus for monitoring	Verbal and written feedback using monitoring sheet
Summer 2	IEP writing and monitoring of progress	SENCO has time with each teacher to look at pupil needs, discuss targets and monitoring strategies in order to feed into review and rewriting of targets	1–1 discussion, written feedback using monitoring sheet and where required follow up meeting

planning, teaching or learning. Figure 4.2 gives a proforma which can be used for recording written feedback following any type of monitoring activity. There is also, in Figure 4.3, an actual example of written feedback to a teacher who had already received considerable support in learning how to use IEPs to improve outcomes for children with SEN, but with limited success. After further face-to-face discussions with senior managers, written feedback was used to make very clear what was expected for improved performance.

Evaluating plans and provision

Evaluation of the impact of school development plans or ongoing SEN provision involves drawing together evidence from a number of sources in order to draw conclusions about how far the work has had the desired effects and has delivered value for money. Evaluation is the tool which leads to decisions about what to do next: whether to go on doing what we have put in place, or do something different. It is the 'review' in the 'plan/do/review' sequence which turns schools into learning organisations able to try out new ideas and methods, test them out through a continuous process of action research, take into the fabric of the organisation those elements which have worked and discard those which have not proved worth the effort that went into them.

The case study below shows how one school planned and carried out a high-quality evaluation involving both quantitative and qualitative methods.

CASE STUDY

Evaluating a school-based speech and language therapy project
The school in this case study had concluded, as a result of self-evaluation, that one reason for low attainment in KS1 and KS2 was the high number of children entering school with underdeveloped language and listening skills. Staff were keen, when the opportunity arose, to take part in a project involving purchase of time from a cluster-based speech and language therapist. The therapist would work with children directly, but also indirectly via work with parents and with school staff, providing training and advice on curriculum planning.

The head teacher, SENCO and therapist, together, determined the targets and actions for the project, which would form part of the school development plan. The main target was an improvement in Key Stage 1 SAT results for the school as a whole, and improved speech and language skills, self-confidence and social interaction for children referred to the project. Since the project was to run over two years, it was particularly important to set milestones, which included:

- evidence of improved planning for speaking and listening skills within long-, medium- and short-term curriculum plans;
- evidence that teaching staff understood more about speech and language development and how best to meet needs;

Date _____   Area/Aspect _____

Class/Age Group _____   By: _____

ACTIVITY

Talking to children	☐	Teacher observation	☐
Display overview	☐	Planning overview	☐
Children's work outline	☐	Other (please state)	☐
Child observation	☐		

Monitoring activity outline

Findings

Proposed future action

Signed _____   _____

Figure 4.2   Primary school monitoring sheet

Date __11.06.02__   Area/Aspect _Special Educational Needs_

Class/Age Group _98 yr. 5/6_   By: _(Deputy HT/SENCO)_

ACTIVITY

Talking to children	☐	Teacher observation	☐
Display overview	☐	Planning overview	☑
Children's work outline	☐	Other (please state)	☐
Child observation	☐		

Monitoring activity outline

Termly review of SEN files in order to monitor:
1) Completion of summer term IEPs   2) Levels of monitoring of pupil progress
3) Parental and pupil involvement   4) Progression in target-setting

---

Findings:

Your IEP targets have shown real improvement and are more specific with success criteria, so well done. However, the majority of your IEPs are unsigned by parents, pupils and often by you. Even where parents are often in school you do not seem to have made contact with them.

Your reviews are still unspecific and rely heavily on '…has made good progress'. There needs to be evidence or data to support the statement. Remember you are reviewing progress towards targets not just making a general comment. Also you often state 'good or excellent progress' yet your class reading standardised assessments, in most cases, showed a regression in achievement. This is why data awareness and close monitoring is essential.

Your monitoring of children's progress towards targets in between reviews is almost non-existent; you will need to do something about this. I will show you monitoring by other staff who have almost the same number of children with SEN and nothing like the same amount of LSA support. Monitoring has to be specific, consistent and systematic.

Proposed future action:

I expect to see monitoring against one target each week for the summer term. See me at SEN surgery next Monday if you are not clear on which sheets you should be using. Each week monitor a different target so they all get covered. Be specific. I will see all your monitoring the week before we break up when I will collect it in to pass on. I expect to see 50% of parents' signatures and 100% from pupils and yourself – thank you.

Signed _____   _____

Figure 4.3   Primary school monitoring sheet

- evidence of parental involvement in planning for and supporting children referred to the project.

Monitoring strategies involved the SENCO in gathering repeated assessment data for the children referred, and in overviewing planning and administering questionnaires to staff and parents. The therapist also planned to film reception class teachers and analyse their use of language, and that of the children, before and after recommended changes of approach/language use/class organisation were made.

The final evaluation, towards the end of the project, was planned right at the start. It would pull together the evidence from questionnaires, SAT and language assessment data, video sequences and teacher planning, in order to draw conclusions about whether the school should continue to invest in shared cluster therapy provision in the long term.

After one year, the SENCO wrote the following interim evaluation:

'Speech and Language Therapy provision has been successfully integrated into the SEN provision made available to pupils in the school. Our link therapist, R, has become a valued member of staff who has offered advice and support to staff, pupils and parents. She has assessed and/or worked with groups and individual children and offered advice to staff/parents regarding 20+ children. She has liaised with staff, contributed to IEPs and devised programmes for LSAs to follow.

Staff completed questionnaires early in the year in order to establish levels of staff knowledge about speech and language needs. As a result of this an INSET day was held during the summer term. This was very successful and led to a number of new children being referred for support. Staff feedback through evaluation sheets and informal discussion showed that staff knowledge and understanding of communication development and strategies for meeting needs had been raised. This feedback has helped in identifying further training needs which will be met through a series of staff meetings throughout next year.

The majority of the children referred for support or teacher advice were from Key Stage 1, in line with our target to raise attainment in this key stage. End-of-year comparisons of autumn and summer baseline assessments showed very pleasing improvements in the area of language: most children had gained at least one level, and in many cases two levels.

On the negative side, the project does not appear to have influenced teacher planning as we would have liked. Monitoring medium- and short-term plans has not as yet shown improved attention to speaking and listening skills. One reason for this may be lack of time for class teachers, SENCO and therapist to meet together.

We had a low return on questionnaires distributed to parents of children involved in the project, and generally failed to achieve the level of parental participation we want to encourage.

Summary and conclusions

School-based evaluation through informal discussion and staff questionnaires has shown a real increase in staff skills and knowledge. This has begun to impact informally on classroom organisation and lesson delivery. We need to follow this up by allocating time now for R to work with us on our planning: beginning by reviewing our schemes of work for speaking and listening, and then taking this into medium- and short-term plans.

We have decided to review our approach to parental involvement. Next year, in addition to the offer of 1–1 meetings with R, we will develop parent groups for those with children in the nursery or reception classes, focusing on early communication development and how children can be supported at home.

It is too early to assess the impact of the project on SAT results at Key Stage 1: this will need ongoing analysis over a number of years in order to evaluate whether we are achieving better value-added outcomes from baseline assessment than we were before we implemented the project. Early results from repeated baseline assessments, however, suggest that the project is successfully improving the communication skills of children directly involved.'

5 | School improvement and SEN: a case study

Introduction

In this chapter we will look at the cycle of planning strategically for school improvement, from self-evaluation through to implementing school development plans, through the eyes of an experienced SENCO and deputy head teacher. The case study is set in a medium-sized primary school with a nursery class, serving an estate where there are very high levels of unemployment, crime and drug misuse. Fifty-six per cent of pupils are eligible for free school meals.

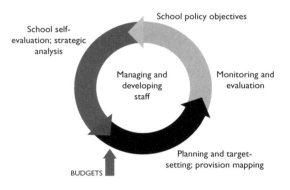

Figure 5.1 The school improvement cycle

A SENCO's story

In my experience I have found that in order to plan strategically for SEN we need to have an ethos or way of thinking which encompasses:

- a recognition of *skills* and the part key staff play in planning for SEN throughout the school;
- an ability to recognise the need for, and embrace, 'joined up thinking', where *strategic planning* at all levels supports the school's vision and aims;
- an understanding of the need for specific *targets focused on the outcomes* of our work on SEN – rather than 'what needs doing'; and
- a collegial attitude to *assessment and monitoring* which informs future planning.

Each of these points of reference demands the involvement of an increasing number of people until all are engaged in the meeting of children's special educational needs. As the Code of Practice (DfES 2001a: 31) makes clear (see

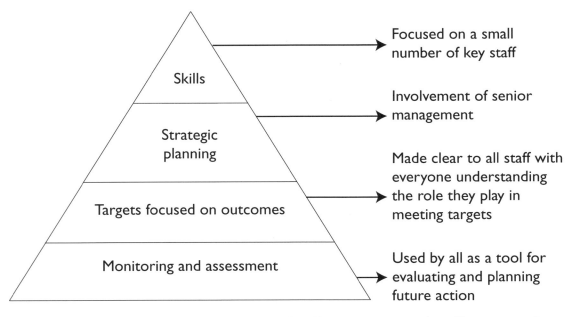

Skills — Focused on a small number of key staff

Strategic planning — Involvement of senior management

Targets focused on outcomes — Made clear to all staff with everyone understanding the role they play in meeting targets

Monitoring and assessment — Used by all as a tool for evaluating and planning future action

Figure 5.2 Progressive involvement of different groups of staff in strategic planning

Figure 5.2): 'Provision for pupils with special educational needs is a matter for the school *as a whole.*'

Developing the skills of key staff

With increased awareness of the need to measure pupil progress, whether this is in academic achievement, behaviour or attendance, the role of the SENCO has become central to the process of strategic planning for school improvement. The SENCO, often with years of experience in the area of special educational needs, has a wealth of knowledge, skills and strategies for working with the most vulnerable children. It is quite clear that the school improvement (or development) plan must include targets relating to SEN. The role of the SENCO must be seen as important as that of the literacy, mathematics or science coordinator. These colleagues are usually members of the senior management team in a school, yet this is not so common in relation to the SENCO.

If SENCOs are to support school strategic planning and play a part in developing the School Improvement Plan, they need to be in a position that affords them the opportunity to see and understand the 'big picture'. They should have an awareness and knowledge of what is happening across the whole school and in all areas that impact upon special educational needs. They need to have access to the range of information and comparative data that comes into school from the LEA and central government. They need to be aware of a range of statutory and non-statutory regulations and guidelines and how these might impact upon current and future processes in school. Above all, they need to have the skills to look at these alongside the needs of the pupils in the school, the skills of staff and the resources available, in order to write strategic plans which move the school community forward in a purposeful way.

In my school, I am Deputy Head and SENCO, and have developed skills at both senior management and special needs levels. However, many SENCOs, despite their considerable skills and knowledge within the field of special education, may not have experience of working on whole-school development planning. There may well be training issues that will need addressing, so that the SENCO is able to participate fully in management discussions. This might be as simple as attending courses which introduce analysis of data (Autumn Packages, PANDA, LEA and national comparative data) or managing strategic planning. Equally, having non-contact time to work alongside other members of the management team or being paired with a senior colleague with skills in this area can offer valuable 'hands-on' training.

Strategic planning

In order to plan strategically it is important to have a clear understanding of how the thinking behind strategic planning, development planning, school improvement and school effectiveness interlink.

- **Strategic planning** involves a focus on long-term objectives which take account of the context and values of the school, incorporating the vision of what the school and the education it provides should look like.
- With clear objectives in mind **School development planning** provides a blueprint for the action to be taken in order to achieve the long-term objectives.
- The action, as outlined in the school development plan, involves a systematic and sustained effort aimed at change in teaching and learning practices and related internal conditions in school. It has the ultimate aim of achieving the objectives and securing **school improvement**. It incorporates a distinct approach to educational change that strengthens the school's capacity for change and enhances outcomes for pupils, ensuring **school effectiveness**.

When looking at strategic planning for SEN I found we needed to ask the following questions, illustrated in Figure 5.3.

When considering strategic planning for SEN we needed to look at a number of factors impacting upon outcomes for children. This includes not only teaching and learning, but also behaviour, attendance, parental involvement and perhaps for some schools, exclusions, pupil mobility or English as a second language. It may be that some of these will intertwine, impacting upon one another, but within each of these areas you should establish priorities for action.

Below, I give some examples of long- term objectives from our SEN strategic plans and how they impact upon a number of areas and practices.

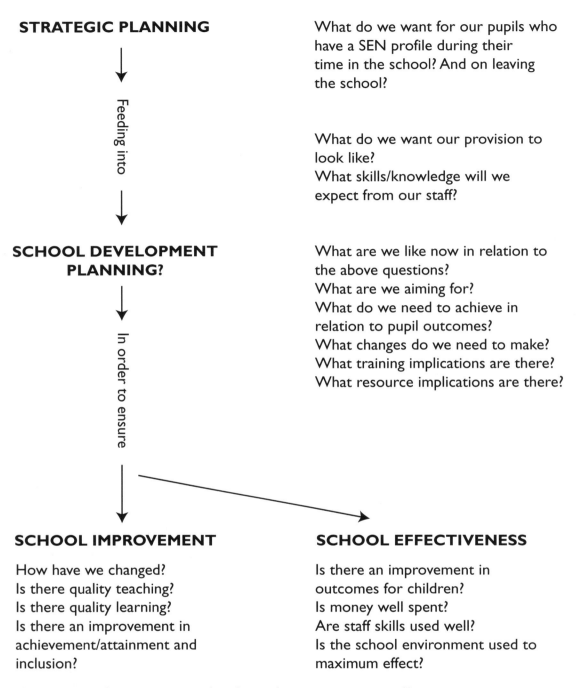

STRATEGIC PLANNING

What do we want for our pupils who have a SEN profile during their time in the school? And on leaving the school?

Feeding into

What do we want our provision to look like?
What skills/knowledge will we expect from our staff?

SCHOOL DEVELOPMENT PLANNING?

What are we like now in relation to the above questions?
What are we aiming for?
What do we need to achieve in relation to pupil outcomes?
What changes do we need to make?
What training implications are there?
What resource implications are there?

In order to ensure

SCHOOL IMPROVEMENT

How have we changed?
Is there quality teaching?
Is there quality learning?
Is there an improvement in achievement/attainment and inclusion?

SCHOOL EFFECTIVENESS

Is there an improvement in outcomes for children?
Is money well spent?
Are staff skills used well?
Is the school environment used to maximum effect?

Figure 5.3 Questions to ask when planning strategically

Targets focused on outcomes

In order to set targets which focus on clear outcomes there needs to be a core practice of data gathering and analysis. I gathered all available data together which gave a SEN baseline and levels of achievement along with other

Table 5.1 Long-term objectives of SEN plans

Focus for strategic planning	Long-term objectives/priorities	impacting upon
Special needs identification	To reduce the number of children requiring support at School Action	identification and provision implementation of catch-up programmes
	To reduce the percentage of boys identified as requiring support at School Action and School Action Plus	staff skills and knowledge teaching and learning reading materials for boys boys in curriculum planning and delivery use of staff skills and time
Attainment	To reduce the percentage < level I in KSI SATs	parental involvement teaching and learning
	To reduce the percentage < level 3 in KS2 SATs	booster provision
	To increase the percentage achieving level 2+ at the end of KSI, and level 4+ at the end of KS2	catch-up and SEN intervention programmes review of resources assessment and data analysis
Behaviour	Reduction in numbers of children gaining 'red cards'	behaviour support strategies staff skills and knowledge deployment of staff
	Reduction in fixed-term exclusions	parental involvement outside agencies
Attendance	To raise overall attendance levels of each class	communication rewards data analysis
	To reduce number of unauthorised absences	SEN/attendance links use of staff time (phoning home on first day of absence)
	To raise the profile of attendance across the school community	parental involvement
Parental involvement	Attendance at Pastoral Support Meetings	communication management of parent consultations open-door ethos
	Attendance at parents' meetings	parental confidence in staff/school understanding of curriculum
	Information to parents	teaching and learning

areas/activities which impact upon achievement falling within the SEN remit, such as attendance, behaviour and parental involvement.

These data on attainment included standardised tests of reading and mathematics and the results of QCA non-statutory tests at Years 3–5. I also looked at data gathered through school systems such as attendance registers,

53

behaviour management strategies and SEN registers/lists. I needed to do a good deal of cross-referencing (for example, poor attendance cross-referenced to children with SEN).

Analysis of data highlighted key areas within each focus that we needed to concentrate on, in order to ensure a holistic impact upon achievement of children identified as having SEN.

Targets were set over a number of years (2000–2004) recognising the variable impact of different cohorts of children and the fact that we needed consistency and persistence and that there was no quick-fix answer. The targets we set, along with the strategies developed to meet them, and our plans for monitoring progress, are shown in Figures 5.4 to 5.7.

Attendance

Data clearly showed that we had an unacceptably high percentage of authorised and unauthorised absences and that the number of children attending school for less than 85 per cent of the time needed to reduce. There was an expectation by the government that attendance should be above 95 per cent, yet weekly data showed that we rarely got above 90 per cent. There was also a clear difference between boys and girls in levels of non-attendance, but not when looking at numbers achieving 100 per cent attendance. We decided to focus energies on authorised and unauthorised absences and those pupils with less than 85 per cent attendance, tightening up on practices and employing a member of staff to telephone home on the first day of absence. We also focused on raising the profile of attendance within the school. The gender differences would be left for the time being.

SEN

Our data showed that we were identifying large numbers of pupils as having SEN – larger than other schools with similar levels of social deprivation. We decided to focus our planning and attention on the development of catch-up programmes in order to impact upon the number of children identified at different levels within the Code of Practice. Within this we would also look at the impact this had upon gender differences. Boys were more likely to be identified as having SEN although they fared a little better as they moved into Key Stage 2.

Attainment

Data highlighted problems across the school with writing and reading. We had a very high percentage of children attaining below level 1 at the end of KS1 – 19.5 per cent in writing in 2000. In our 2000 KS2 English results we had 32 per cent of the cohort below level 3 – though we had begun to close the gap between ourselves and similar schools in the time since I became SENCO, when the figure was as high as 36 per cent. We therefore planned to invest heavily in literacy interventions: Phonographix in Years 1–3, and Reading Recovery at Years 1–2. In Key Stage 2 we planned to make the national Additional Literacy Support and Further Literacy Support (ALS and FLS)

Priority

1. To reduce the number of children identified as requiring support at School Action and School Action Plus

2. To reduce the number of children identified as having SEN

3. To reduce the percentage of boys identified as requiring SEN support at School Action and School Action Plus

Targets

1. An overall reduction of the number of children identified as having SEN at School Action and School Action Plus by 1.5% each year

2. A reduction in the number and percentage of children identified as having SEN across all levels of support by 2% each year

3. A reduction in the differentials between boys and girls by 0.5% each year, as a percentage figure of all children identified

Strategies

❑ Focused use of catch-up programmes at both Key Stages implemented by teachers and LSAs
❑ Increased involvement of SENCO working at Key Stage 1
❑ Increased parental involvement through development of parent courses
❑ Clear criteria for supporting children at SA and SA+ levels
❑ Whole-school approach to social skills and self-esteem ('You can do it') and use of accelerated learning strategies, particularly where they promote boys learning

Monitoring – by SENCO (reporting termly to governors)

❑ Maintenance of SEN and Inclusion lists and statistics
❑ Termly overview of IEP monitoring
❑ SENCO and LEA SEN support service review and monitoring of implementation and success of catch-up programmes (particularly for boys)
❑ SENCO and LEA SEN support service review and monitoring of impact of interventions/strategies in raising pupil self-esteem and social skills (particularly for boys)
❑ SENCO discussion with teaching staff of the impact that work of LEA SEN support service has on teaching strategies and on children's learning

Milestones

❑ Children move down to School Action or Classroom Differentiation level of need after a period of targeted intervention
❑ Staff are confident of their assessment and decisions in moving children down through levels of support required

Figure 5.4 Primary school SEN targets 2000–2004

Priority

1. Annual attendance percentage

2. Number of children with less than 85% attendance

3. Level of unauthorised absence

Targets

1. 91% attendance by July 2002, rising by 0.5% each subsequent year

2. No more than 10% of the total pupils having attendance at less than 85%

3. Reduction of unauthorised absences to 1.5% by 2004

Strategies

❑ First day phone call for all pupils with less than 85% attendance
❑ EWO/parent coffee mornings to discuss attendance issues
❑ Weekly attendance assemblies
❑ Certificates/rewards for best class attendance, pupil 100% attendance and improved attendance
❑ Termly leaflet to parents raising profile of attendance
❑ Roles and responsibilities made clear to new parents at Reception entry meetings in summer term
❑ Termly multi-disciplinary meetings have attendance as an item for discussion

---

Monitoring

❑ SENCO – weekly/half-termly/termly/annual collection and monitoring of data
❑ Key LSA – daily scrutiny of register and first day phone call, overview of late book
❑ Clerical staff – upkeep of late book
❑ EWO and SENCO – overview of registers and children whose attendance is cause for concern
❑ Governors – through report to governors at termly governor meetings

---

Milestones

❑ More children gain certificates for 100% attendance each term
❑ Parents make contact with the school to explain why their children are away
❑ At least one class each month has 98% attendance
❑ Number of children on cause for concern list slowly reduces
❑ Fewer children are discussed at multi-disciplinary meetings

Figure 5.5   Primary school attendance targets 2000–2004

Priority

1. Below level 1 attainment in Key Stage 1 SATs

2. Below level 3 attainment in Key Stage 2 SATs

3. Cohort 2000–2001 (Reception) Key Stage 1 SAT prediction 2003

4. Cohort 1997–1998 (Year 4) Key Stage 2 SAT prediction 2003

Targets

1. 3% reading/10% writing/5% maths below level 1 at the end of Key Stage 1

2. 10% English/8% maths below level 3 at the end of Key Stage 2

3. Reading 70%/writing 70%/maths 70% level 2+ at the end of Key Stage 1

4. English 55%/maths 55%/science 65% level 4+ at the end of Key Stage 2

Strategies

❑ Focused use of catch-up programmes and SEN interventions at both key stages implemented by teachers and LSAs
❑ Increased involvement of SENCO working across Key Stage 1
❑ Regular setting of targets for and with children/parents
❑ Planned and co-ordinated booster teaching at nursery, Reception, Year 1, Year 2, Year 5 and Year 6

Monitoring

❑ Class teacher – termly pupil tracking sheets
❑ Year band leaders – monthly overview of planning and differentiation
❑ SENCO – overview of IEPs and monitoring to targets
❑ SENCO – termly assessment of key pupils
❑ SENCO and LEA SEN support service – review and monitoring of catch-up programmes and SEN interventions
❑ Assessment coordinator, head teacher and SMT – annual data analysis

---

Milestones

❑ Targeted groups complete catch-up programmes and SEN interventions
❑ 98% children are successfully discontinued from Reading Recovery after 12–20 weeks
❑ Termly pupil tracking sheets show pupils on track to reach targets

---

Figure 5.6   Primary school attainment targets 2000–2004

Priority

1. Children gaining red cards

2. Exclusions – fixed term

Targets

1. 25% reduction in annual total of red cards year on year

2. 10% reduction in number of children experiencing fixed-term exclusions year on year

---

Strategies

❑ Focused Pastoral Support Plan meetings for children at risk of exclusion
❑ Close liaison with parents
❑ Appropriate and prompt use of outside agencies
❑ Lunchtime alternatives – red/yellow card rooms, activity room
❑ LSAs on duty through lunchtime
❑ Senior staff on duty during lunchtime
❑ 'You can do it' social skills/self-esteem programme throughout school
❑ Weekly achievement certificates and 'You can do it' certificates
❑ Termly multi-disciplinary team meetings to discuss strategies and review needs/progress

---

Monitoring

❑ Senior Teacher – collection and analysis of red/yellow card data
❑ SENCO – Pastoral Support Planning, review and monitoring of timescales and successes
❑ Head teacher – collection and overview of exclusion data
❑ Key LSAs – Yellow card data collection and feedback to senior staff
❑ Multi-disciplinary team – termly review of progress and children's needs
❑ SMT – Termly analysis of data

Milestones

❑ Frequency of major incidents is reduced
❑ Fewer children have Pastoral Support Plans
❑ Term on term reduction in red cards
❑ Staff perceptions of improved behaviour

Figure 5.7 Primary school behaviour targets 2000–2004

programmes available in modified form to children identified at School Action, and not simply those we wanted to boost from level 3 to level 4+.

Within a year or so it was clear that our progress in maths was suffering and as a result strategies were added (focus on mental maths, reviewing teaching strategies and refocus on how Springboard programmes were used) in order to tackle this area too.

Behaviour

Data analysed referred to behaviour support systems set up within school, major incidents of inappropriate behaviours and number of exclusions. We found that we had relatively high numbers of fixed-term exclusions, and even more 'unofficial' internal exclusions, where children were spending long periods in the head teacher's office as the only way of containing their behaviour and keeping them in school. A whole-school review of behaviour management strategies and communication systems was carried out in order to impact upon these figures.

Monitoring and assessment

Having gathered and analysed data in order to establish needs and set targets, it is crucial to maintain this gathering and analysis regime throughout the year, supported by monitoring of the day-to-day strategies employed, in order to judge the impact actions are making. It is very easy to feel satisfied by planned action, but ultimately it must have an impact upon outcomes. Strategic planning is no more than a paper exercise unless processes are in place to monitor the intervention and action, and assess what happens as a result.

This is not simply the role of the SENCO, nor the senior management team; it needs to be part of the repertoire of all staff in planning for and delivering a quality curriculum within a supportive learning community.

The SENCO's role will be advising and leading staff regarding strategies for monitoring and assessing the impact of the school's planning and provision on pupils with special educational needs. S/he can provide a clear knowledge of what data is required and how it will be analysed, ensuring a cyclical approach to planning.

Evaluation

A review of our targets showed improvements, but also areas where it appeared no impact was evident. The numbers of children identified as having SEN was not reducing: it seemed that staff had a picture of the proportion of their class they felt were struggling, which remained more or less constant despite improvements in actual attainment and behaviour. We discussed this as a staff group and agreed that there were probably some perverse incentives at work here, through our systems for allocating additional LSA time based on numbers of children with identified SEN in each class. All could see that we were making a rod for our own backs by the over-identification of individuals

Table 5.2 Key Stage One (below level 1)

Year	Reading		Writing		Maths	
	Target	Actual	Target	Actual	Target	Actual
1999		7.5% (LEA 5.2%)		27.5% (LEA 9.3%)		5% (LEA 3.9%)
2000		4.9% (LEA 3.9%)		19.5% (LEA 7.2%)		12.2% (LEA 3.5%)
2001	6%	12.8% (LEA 3.9%)	12%	15.3% (LEA 5.6%)	9%	7.6% (LEA 2.5%)
2002	4%	7.6% (LEA 5.8%)	10%	7.8% (LEA 6.6%)	6%	0% (LEA 4.1%)
2003	2%		8%		4%	
2004	0%		5%		2%	

at the expense of inclusive teaching strategies for all: we agreed to review and improve the criteria we used for placing children on School Action as a first step.

In relation to attendance, evaluation showed that we had not met our target of reducing the number of children identified as having less that 85 per cent attendance. Overall levels of attendance were showing improvements, however. We seemed to have been successful in changing attitudes to attendance in the wider community, but not touched the core of families experiencing acute social stress, disorganization and alienation.

In relation to attainment we were able to show some substantial improvements, particularly in writing and maths in Key Stage 1 (Table 5.2).

In behaviour we found that the percentage of pupils having at least one fixed-term exclusion had reduced from 6.5 per cent in 1999 to 3.2 per cent in 2002. The total days lost to fixed-term exclusion, however, had remained more or less constant. Interviews with staff suggested that they felt that overall behaviour had improved in the school, with fewer children acting up. What had not changed was the core of children with very disturbed behaviour, several of whom had repeated and lengthy exclusions while we sought help for them. It was this which meant that the total days lost to exclusion had not reduced. We are optimistic, however, about having more impact on these children and their families in future, as we are now involved in a number of multiagency initiatives brought about through the Children's Fund and the national Behaviour Improvement Project.

Table 5.3   Primary school coordinator's long-term planning sheet

An overview of plans to review/update/renew practices in key areas of the school in order to raise achievement		
Subject/Priority Area: Special Educational Needs		**Coordinator:** _____
Strategic area	**2002–2003**	**2003–2004**
Teaching and learning	▪ Highlight/raise profile of strategies and resources encouraging independent learning ▪ Review/monitor catch-up programmes ▪ Phonographix info. to all staff	▪ Review/maintain/extend catch-up programmes ▪ Monitor opportunities for and impact of independent learning
Curriculum	▪ Promote literacy support strategies through class based book corners ▪ Raise profile of ICT re. SEN ▪ Further develop Reading Recovery (RR) at KS1 ▪ Staff meeting at RR centre	▪ Develop maths corners with clear labelling and handy hints ▪ Reference accelerated learning as strategy for supporting SEN
Children and the community	▪ Promote attendance to pupils / parents and community ▪ Promote strategies for pupil target setting ▪ Trial 'reading with children' in Year 1 ▪ Monitor parental involvement	▪ Promote 'reading with children' in order to encourage more voluntary helpers in Key Stage 1
Environment	▪ Reliable resource base ▪ Possibility of SEN base/groupwork base at KS1? ▪ Promote classroom organisation re. independent learning ▪ Parental involvement in making/ repairing resources	▪ Review layout of SEN base(s)
Management	▪ Revisit monitoring of IEP targets ▪ Timetable time for staff to speak with teachers from LEA SEN support service ▪ SENCO/support service liaison to review catch-up programmes/use of staff ▪ Ratify SEN Policy (governors)	▪ Review strategies re. independent learning

Managing my role in school improvement

To keep track of my part in implementing and monitoring our school development plans, I found I needed some kind of overview of activity over the year as a whole, and within each term. I therefore devised a simple grid of my planned activities under the headings teaching and learning, curriculum, children and the community, the learning environment and management tasks.

Table 5.4   Coordinator's yearly planning sheet 2002–2003

Subject/Priority Area: Special Educational Needs		Coordinator: _____	
Strategic area	**Autumn Term**	**Spring Term**	**Summer Term**
Teaching and learning	▪ Clarify catch-up progs In use and by/with whom ▪ Establish baseline to monitor progs against ▪ Phonographix info. to all	▪ Monitor pupil progress re. catch-up programmes ▪ Raise profile of strategies for independent learning	▪ Review catch-up programmes used and plan for next year
Curriculum	▪ Further develop RR at KSI ▪ Establish progs/groups for KS2 SEN teacher ▪ Staff meeting at RR base	▪ Audit SEN resources ▪ Raise profile of ICT and SEN ———→	▪ Specifically review KS2 catch-up progs
Children and the community	▪ High-profile attendance ▪ Consider school requirements re. pupil targets ▪ Monitor parental involvement	▪ Trial 'reading with children' in Year ▪ Publish handbook *'Reading with children'* ▪ High-profile strategies for pupil targets ——→	▪ Discuss parental involvement with school council
Environment	▪ Re-label SEN base resources	▪ Review resource accessibility ▪ Highlight strategies to promote independent learning ———→	▪ Consider possibility of dedicated group SEN room at Key Stage I
Management	▪ Report to Govs ——————→ ▪ Policy to Govs ▪ Timetable LEA SEN support service involvement (pupils and staff) ▪ Children's Fund ——	▪ Revisit monitoring to IEP targets ▪ Review staff ——→ involvement with catch-up programmes	——→

The grid (Tables 5.3 and 5.4) has proved invaluable both as a prompt for immediate actions and as a tool for thinking strategically over a longer period about the key tasks to which I need to allocate time if we are to achieve our goals.

6 Planning provision: using a provision map

Introduction

As we have seen in previous chapters, SEN has a part in the cycle of self-evaluation, school development planning and target-setting which is similar to that of any other aspect of school business. In this chapter, however, we will look at an aspect of strategic management that is unique to SEN – not replicated in other school improvement domains.

This aspect, planning the provision which the school will make each year for pupils with SEN and disabilities, runs in parallel with preparing the School Development (or Improvement) Plan. It follows the school's annual autumn self-evaluation, is informed (heavily) by budgetary considerations and is likely to be undertaken in the spring term ready for implementation in the new school year.

Planning provision for pupils with SEN has in the past been one of the least strategic of all aspects of SEN management. In smaller schools, the provision has often been felt to depend on funding allocated to individual pupils by the LEA, on a fairly random timescale, with no more planning involved than adding an hour or two to the work of an existing part-time learning support assistant, or recruiting a new one for a few hours a week. In other schools, which do make some SEN provision within their establishment, planning may have depended on the amount of money left over when other calls on the budget have been met, and on who might be available to take on the work.

Many schools, however, are now adopting a more considered approach, in a climate where LEAs are required to make clear the funding available within schools' budgets for School Action, and the obligation on schools to provide it.

Another impetus for a strategic approach is the continuing growth in the numbers of teaching assistants employed in schools from various funding sources, and the consequent need for schools to take decisions on how best to deploy their assistants in pursuit of agreed priorities.

BUDGETS

provision mapping

Figure 6.1 The school improvement cycle

Determining SEN priorities

The factors which will help determine your school priorities for deploying additional adult support for pupils with SEN include:

- your self-evaluation of strengths and weaknesses in the attainment and inclusion of pupils with SEN;
- information about 'what works' in provision for pupils with SEN;
- pupil needs analysis; and
- budgetary information.

In Chapter 3 we saw how **self-evaluation** (both quantitative and qualitative) works to identify areas where the school is doing well, and areas where it could improve. Such evaluation might indicate a need, for example, for reshaped SEN provision in a particular key stage, year group, subject area or SEN need area such as autism or behaviour.

Later on, in Chapter 7, we will look at information about **what works** in provision for pupils with SEN.

The process of **pupil needs analysis** – projecting numbers with particular types of special need, in each year group, so as to be aware of future trends – was described in Chapter 2. At the stage of planning provision for the year ahead, you will need to do this in more detail. The SENCO will want to pull together a list of all known children who would benefit from additional provision (including those starting school or transferring from other schools), and jot down the type of provision they require using a must-should-could classification and a grid such as the one in Table 6.1.

In the 'must' rows of the grid go the names of children for whom specific types of provision are statutory: that is, children with a Statement of SEN. Against their names go ticks or a number of hours (if specified on the Statement) in each relevant type of provision column. In the 'should' row go the names of children who have the next highest call on available provision, because of the severity of their needs, the impact of those needs on other learners, or their rate of progress. Assessment information, including the most recent IEPs, is used to add ticks to show the type of provision they require. The 'could' row is for other children – and it will always be a long list – for whom the school would want to make additional provision if it can.

Next comes budgetary information, shared between the head teacher, the bursar if there is one, SENCO and governor with responsibility for SEN. Where local funding systems allow, the available budgets for SEN should be aggregated rather than managed as separate funding streams for Statements, LEA SEN audits, elements of Standards Funding directed at inclusion or tackling behaviour difficulties, school funding for additional educational needs, and a proportion of the age-weighted pupil unit – or any of the other systems in place in the area.

Aggregation of funding streams allows schools to move away from arranging support on an ad hoc basis through individually allocated learning support assistant hours, to a more strategic and planned approach. It allows

Table 6.1 Planning provision – year group

	Name of child	Structured literacy programme	Structured numeracy programme	Structured language programme	Coordination programme	1–1 counselling	SEBD groupwork	In-class support	Modification of curriculum presentation	Other
MUST										
SHOULD										
COULD										

the school to move away from piecemeal planning of provisions that do not work in a coherent way – a Learning Support Unit (LSU) staffed by a teacher and a teaching assistant with a high degree of expertise to support pupils with behaviour difficulties but 'without SEN', for example, while large numbers of pupils on School Action for EBD receive other forms of support from less skilled staff elsewhere. It allows the school to audit children's needs across the piece, and then map out a coherent plan for targeting funding to meet them. It also helps to prevent a common pattern of over-provision in some classes or year groups, and under-provision in others: a large amount of extra adult support in one year group, for example (funded variously via Statements, school SEN funding, funds used for NLS and NNS or Key Stage 3 Strategy 'catch up' intervention programmes, or Excellence in Cities mentoring arrangements), and much less in other year groups, or a number of adults in one class with different support roles and no additional support at all in the class next door.

The outcomes of school self-evaluation and the audit of pupil needs will tell the school what provision it might make in order to provide for pupils who need additional help with their learning or behaviour. The box below shows the conclusions that one secondary school might come to about the provision it needed.

Our audit of pupil need and our self-evaluation tells us that next year we will need:

- someone who can offer group work to children with SEBD, particularly in Years 8 and 9;
- someone with counselling skills;
- a way of helping subject staff with differentiation;
- someone who can run maths groups in Year 7;
- someone who can run literacy groups in Year 7;
- a way of pulling together support packages for a projected increase in numbers of children with complex physical impairments entering the school, which has recently been made accessible via a building programme;
- people to pull together the packages of support required by other children with SEN – one 'key worker' per year group, with excellent organisational skills;
- as much in-class support as can possibly be afforded, targeted at Year 7 as a first, early intervention priority, and at a very difficult Year 9 group as the second priority;
- specific personal assistant support for several individual children with physical and sensory impairments.

The school would then combine its various funding streams for SEN and behaviour and set aside a 'buffer' sum in case pupils with earmarked individual funding (for example, with Statements) should leave in the course of the year, taking their funding with them. The remaining amount would be used to cost a provision map based on the priorities in the box above: starting with the more specialised forms of provision and using any remaining sums to fund learning support assistants to provide in-class support.

This system also allows the school to plan staffing. The SENCO was able to identify where there were already skills available within the school (a literacy specialist, a maths specialist, a number of excellent organisers and a teacher with particular skills in preparing and adapting teaching resources, for example) and where there might be a need to recruit – for a trained counsellor, an EBD specialist and a teacher with expertise in the area of physical impairment, or at least a willingness to undergo specialist training in this area.

Drawing up a provision map

Having costed a proposed new pattern of provision, the next step is to draw up a Provision Map, detailing the range of support which the school will give to children with SEN in each of its year groups. Provision maps, illustrated in Tables 6.2 and 6.3, are a convenient way of documenting school provision. They make it easy for schools to set out, in their annual governors' report to parents, the resources that have been available and the ways in which they have been used.

They also help schools to cost their provision accurately. This can be difficult, when staff (such as learning support assistants) are involved in both SEN and non-SEN activities. Provision maps allow you to separate out SEN activities by allocating hours per week to each activity, and using ready-reckoners for staff costings (available from your LEA) to turn the total hours into weekly, then annual, costs.

Provision maps are also a very effective way of showing the provision a school is making for individual children. The particular pattern of support a child is receiving can be highlighted, or ticked with the amount of time per week added (Table 6.4). Attached to a set of targets, it can form part of the IEP (showing strategies to be used and the roles and responsibilities of staff involved) for the child, and will save you having to write these out over and over again for groups of children. Parents can see at a glance what will be happening with their child; if the provisions are all costed out, they can see what is being spent by the school to meet their child's needs. Provision maps have also proved useful at Tribunals to demonstrate the overall pattern of support which a school can provide, so that this can be compared with alternatives.

Finally, provision maps are very helpful in planning for an age progression in provision for children with SEN. One of the common mistakes in planning SEN provision is to put in support which, though effective in itself, fails to motivate children because it is repetitive, not age-appropriate, and makes them feel bad about themselves. Year after year of the same reading scheme, the same spelling software, the same pattern of behaviour targets and rewards, or of one-to-one counselling can make children feel they are stuck at the same stage and not making progress. As with any learning they need variety, and effective planning needs to make sure there is a clear progression in the types of activities they are offered.

Provision maps will allow you to check whether such a progression is in place in your school. At a glance, you will be able to see from a map where you might need to introduce some variety, which year groups might need to take a break from a particular scheme or programme, which activities seem

Table 6.2 Example of a primary school provision map

Year	Provision/resource	Cost (per week)
Nursery	■ Daily language support based around regular nursery activities ■ Teaching to individual targets based on Portage model of assessment and intervention ■ Home school book bags/suggested activities around sharing a book ■ Parenting group	5 hour NNEB
Reception	■ Daily speaking and listening programme with nursery nurse using, e.g. appropriate section of the Teaching Talking handbook ■ Small group phonological awareness programme (Sound Beginnings) ■ Nurture group placement	2.5 hour NNEB 2.5 hour teaching assistant (TA) Full-time teacher
Years 1/2	■ ICT, e.g. Animated Alphabet ■ 15 minutes a day literacy and numeracy programmes ■ Individual reward system ■ SMSA support during lunchtime	5 hour TA
Years 3/4	■ ICT, e.g. Talking Pen Down, Wordshark ■ Phono-graphix™ group ■ Modified ALS catch up programme ■ Social skills group	1 hour SENCO 2.5 hour TA 1 hour SENCO 2.5 hour TA 1 hour Deputy Head
Years 5/6	■ Lunchtime library group ■ Homework club and family literacy project ■ Precision teaching – maths ■ Play reading group using, e.g. Penguin Plays ■ Phono-graphix group ■ Paired reading with an older mentor (Year 10 from local secondary schools) ■ Behaviour log and reward system ■ Circle of Friends ■ Individual counselling	5 hour library assistant External funding 3 hours TA Volunteer helper 1 hour SENCO 1 hour SENCO 20 minutes per day TA 1 hour SENCO 1 hour per week from LEA support service

This is an example of a provision map for a medium-sized primary school in an area of high social deprivation. In the nursery class, a number of children have been identified as having difficulties with language and listening skills. Several children are showing substantial developmental delay in a number of areas. Staff in the nursery have had Portage training and are able to use this to work in the nursery and with parents on individual weekly targets for these children. The nursery staff also use 'book bags' which encourage parents and carers to share picture books with their children, and follow up each book with simple home-based activities. There is a thriving parent group, meeting weekly to discuss ways of managing common behaviour problems. In reception, the school has set up a special nurture group, where up to twelve children at a time receive support for two to three terms in the skills they need for learning – outside the nurture group, two children have a daily speaking and listening programme, for half an hour a day, with a TA. A group of six children work with an LSA twice a week during the Literacy Hour, on activities and games to develop their phonological awareness. By Years 1 and 2 some children are still only making very slow progress with reading. Those who can with a little help 'catch up' with their peers are placed on the NLS Early Literacy Support Programme. Children with a greater level of need work on a 1–1 programme for 15 minutes a day with a TA. A similar programme operates for mathematics. Individual reward systems are in place for several children with behaviour difficulties, and a school meals supervisory assistant (SMSA) takes a small group each lunchtime for organised playground games. When children move into Key Stage 2 they are able to join social skills groups, run by a teacher with help from the local behaviour support service. These groups run for six weeks at a time and cover friendship skills, managing conflict and angry feelings, and assertiveness skills. Children with literacy difficulties can access the Phono-graphix™ programme. There is much use of ICT for children with special needs. In Years 5 and 6 there is a paired reading scheme organised in conjunction with the local secondary school. The secondary school arranges for some of its disaffected Year 10 pupils to 'mentor' younger pupils, visiting regularly to read with them. There is also a lunchtime literacy group for extra reading; a small number of children are on a daily precision teaching scheme to help them learn a basic sight vocabulary and phonic skills. Children with persisting emotional and behavioural difficulties may become part of a 'Circle of Friends', or meet regularly with a teacher from the behaviour support service for individual counselling. Throughout the school, some children who are supported by this range of provisions will be Statemented; most will not. For the Statemented children there may be extra provision (usually in-class support) which meets their very individual needs. For the most part, however, they will slot into the pattern of group provisions (social skills groups, nurture groups, structured literacy programmes) alongside other non-Statemented children. In this way the school is able to make maximum use of its limited resources, meeting needs effectively but also economically.

Table 6.3   Extract from a secondary school provision map

Year group	Provision/resource	Cost (per week)
7	Nurture base for 10 pupils	Full-time support teacher
	In-class support LSA	30 hours LSA
	English/literacy group	$4\frac{1}{2}$ x 50 mins (max 8) x 4 groups – support teacher
	Registration reading/Phono-graphix " " "	(2 pupils) 4 x 20 mins support teacher (2 pupils) 4 x 20 mins LSA
	Literacy withdrawal (Dyslexia)	(4 pupils) 1 x 50 mins support teacher
	Touch typing (registration)	(2 pupils) 2 x 20 mins LSA
	Lunch/break Haven	(Average 12 pupils) 5 x 1 hour 20 mins LSA and support teacher
	Social skills base	(4 pupils) 1 x 50 mins EBD support teacher
	Access to spellchecker, laptop with voice activated software	Resource purchase annually (£1,200)
	Buddy system Yr 7/Yr 12	2 hours LSA organisation time
10	Literacy groups	4 x 50 mins x 4 groups (4 pupils) – support teacher
	Study support groups	2 x 50 mins x groups (8 pupils) – support teacher
	Part-time college placements	Annual cost £2,720
	Alternative curriculum Group 1 – Youth Awards, Junior Wheels, Work related learning	15 x 50 mins (10 pupils) support teacher
	Alternative Curriculum Group 2 – ditto	6 x 50 mins (10 pupils) support teacher
	Anger management group	(4 pupils) 1 x 50 mins EBD support teacher
	Access to spellchecker, laptop etc.	Resource purchase Annually (£1,200)
	In-class support	LSA 26 x 50 mins
	Certificate of Achievement Course (En) " " " (Ma)	Extra teacher to run small set " " "

This shows an extract from a secondary school's provision map. It sets out the withdrawal groups that the Learning Support Department operates (literacy and social skills groups), and the help given to pupils using ICT. Lunchtime has been recognised as a 'hot spot' for many pupils with SEN, and the Department operates a lunchtime haven, staffed by a teacher and a learning support assistant, where children can go to use computers and take part in organised activities. Alternative curricula have been developed for pupils in Key Stage 4, and these too are recorded on the provision map.

Table 6.4   Provision map for Adam, who is in Year 3

Year	Provision/resource	Provision for Adam
Nursery	➤ Daily language support based around regular nursery activities ➤ Home-school book bags/suggested activities around sharing a book	
Reception	➤ Daily speaking and listening programme with nursery nurse using, e.g. appropriate section of the 'Teaching Talking' handbook ➤ Small group phonological awareness programme	
Yrs 1/2	➤ LSA support using structured phonics programme ➤ Reading Recovery programme	
Yrs 3/4	➤ Individual 'Talking Pen Down' session with LSA daily ➤ 'Catch-Up' Programme ➤ Social skills group	√ 5x20 mins Mrs B √ I hr/week Mr S Mon after play
Yrs 5/6	➤ Lunchtime library group ➤ Portable computer project ➤ Paired reading ➤ 20 mins a day on Toe-by-Toe ➤ Individual behaviour plan	
This is an example of a primary school provision map which has been attached to an IEP to show the provision being made for Adam, a Year 3 child with literacy and social, emotional and behavioural difficulties.		

age-appropriate and which might be seen by children as repetitive or inappropriate for their age group.

CASE STUDY

Provision mapping

At first sight, the thought of drawing together a provision map can be daunting. You will have questions in your mind such as how to start, what to put in it, how to link provision and costing and how to present it in a way that makes it an informative and useful document.

In approaching this task in my school I was determined to stick to my belief that managing and planning for special educational needs is not just the job of the SENCO. However, the approach taken needed to be led by me. So I began by focusing on some key questions:

• What do we want our provision map to look like?
• Who is it for and what is it for?
• What support do we offer at the moment?
• What roles do staff play in this?

- What roles do outside agencies play?
- What skills, knowledge and experience in relation to SEN do our staff have?
- How do we spend and allocate our SEN budgets overall?
- What specific costings can we identify in relation to support for pupils?

Making the provision explicit

Our first thoughts in relation to these questions were that the map would be a list of what the children might have access to as they experienced different levels of need in moving through our school, with some indication of the level of adult support that might go with it. We felt the map should show some sort of progression through the school and should indicate to parents what was on offer and when children might access it. We also knew that by linking money to it we would be able to show how we were spending our SEN budgets. However, on reflection I felt this was far too simplistic, open to being no more than a paper exercise. I believed we had very skilled staff who used many strategies to support children with special needs, and that as a school we had developed many preventative systems to pre-empt both learning and behaviour difficulties. I wanted our provision map to reflect this and to make clear that we were a school that planned support at all levels. I wanted our provision map to demonstrate layered thinking that when put together would make our SEN provision explicit.

Describing and evidencing our provision as part of our SEN Policy would include:

- an overview or statement of our SEN planning and provision, clarifying
  - a view of the nature and frequency of SEN,
  - how we support pupil development,
  - human resourcing and funding,
- use of skills, knowledge and expertise of staff and involvement of outside agencies;
- a visual map of our provision;
- the match of action to levels of need; and
- provision costings.

I then needed to think about the audiences for the map, and the process we should use to arrive at a first draft.

Provision Maps

Who for?	Who involved?
• Parents – gives a clear message that their child's needs are important and provision is part of a whole-school planning strategy.	• Headteacher and SENCO in collaboration with
	– senior management team
• LEA/OFSTED – shows that funding is well used and targeted within a coherent plan for SEN provision.	– all staff
	– outside agencies
	– LEA (where necessary)

- SENCO – provides a succinct overview of provision and how it is to be managed.
- Class teacher – clarifies the support the SEN children in their class could access and roles and responsibilities.

With this in mind, I began by involving all staff in a review and acknowledgement of what we did and what strategies we used to support pupils with SEN throughout the day, and what roles different groups of staff played in the overall picture. This was not as easy a task as I had imagined. Staff were so used to their good practice that they no longer saw them as strategies, or were so used to key resources that they no longer saw them as special. We have set up many supportive systems for managing children with challenging behaviour, and staff took this as normal, rather than us as a school meeting a very real need in our children. As a result they tended to focus narrowly on outside agency support and specific withdrawal for specialised activities rather than really looking at what the children were experiencing.

As a result I decided to go back to staff and ask them to think about what they would do or ask for, if a new child started in their class who had the following needs:

- difficulties with any aspect of literacy or numeracy;
- challenging behaviours;
- speech and language difficulties;
- physical or medical difficulties.

Staff were also asked to focus on what whole-school systems and strategies we had in place, and what advice and expertise they would get from within school and outside agencies.

This gave them a clearer focus and generated greater discussion. It also helped in identifying continuity and progression through SEN provision. This was then all transferred to a provision map against year group and level of need (Table 6.5). We also felt it important to indicate the range of provision that children with lower levels of special need might receive and as such our provision map shows support and strategies across normal classroom differentiation through to School Action and School Action Plus. In addition, we matched action taken by the school to levels of need, clarifying how assessment and planning was carried out, grouping for teaching purposes, use of staff and curriculum and teaching methods that might be used (Table 6.6).

Costing the provision
Once you have made clear your SEN provision you are more able to match costs to it. It is important to clarify exactly what money comes into the school budget, either earmarked for special needs or with an expectation that a percentage will

Table 6.5a Primary school SEN provision map 2002–2003 Foundation Stage, Years 1 and 2

Year	In-class specific differentiation strategies	School Action	School Action Plus
Nursery	Nursery Nurse time for: • Daily language support based around regular nursery activities • Circle Time focused on social emotional skill needs identified through assessment	• Daily speaking and listening programme using, e.g. LEA Language Intervention programme • Teaching to individual targets based on developmental model of assessment and intervention • SENCO support in Nursery for assessment and intervention • Individualised behaviour support (based on LEA behaviour screening and intervention package)	• Speech and Language Therapy advice • LEA SEN support service advice supporting nursery language group • School nurse advice
Reception	Enhanced LSA support for: • Regular group teaching lit/num • Roll & write activities • Handwriting programme linked to Jolly Phonics • Basic skills over-learning • Jolly Phonics alphabet/sound games/sheets • Oxford Reading Tree activities • Pencil grips	Enhanced LSA support for: • Specific group teaching lit/num • Specific 1–1 teaching to targets • Story sack language work • Individualised behaviour programme (based on LEA behaviour screening and intervention package) • SENCO individual/group support as required • SENCO informal assessment • Time out lunchtime support	• Speech & Language Therapy 1–1/group work • LSA language group (Makaton) • LEA SEN support service observation and advice/input to IEPs • Mental health nurse counselling • Attendance worker
Year 1/2	Enhanced LSA support for: • Regular group teaching lit/num • Basic skills over-learning • Sunshine Spiral games • Phonics handbook sheets • Charles Cripps 'Hand for Spelling' activities • LDA language cards • Sound Links – segmenting cards • Class linked SMSA • Early Literacy Support (ELS)	Enhanced LSA support for: • Small group teaching lit/numeracy • Specific 1–1 teaching to targets • Phono-graphix groupwork. • Phono-graphix 1–1 • SENCO led Reading Recovery approach to literacy groupwork • Soundworks/Numberworks • Time-out lunchtime support • Individualised behaviour programme • Specific teaching to targets • Stile Listening Lotto activities • SENCO individual/group support as required • SENCO assessment • LSA language group • Reading Recovery 1–1	• Speech & Language Therapy 1–1/group work • LEA SEN support service observation and advice/input to IEPs • Mental health nurse counselling • Attendance worker

Table 6.5b Primary school SEN provision map 2002–2003 Years 3 and 4

Year	In-class specific differentiation strategies	School Action	School Action Plus
Year 3/4	Enhanced LSA support for: • Regular group teaching lit/num • Easy Learn worksheets • Lit/num games from SEN base • Paired reading • Abacus Maths support activities • Charles Cripps 'Hand for Spelling' • Group topic mats (laminated A3 sheets with key words, diagrams, mind maps, picture cues to support independent learning) • Group literacy mats • Group numeracy mats • Springboard Maths • Additional Literacy Support (ALS)	• Small group teaching lit/numeracy, using, e.g. Soundworks and Numberworks programmes, Word Shark (ICT), Number Shark (ICT), Eye for Spelling (ICT),Wizards Spelling programme, Stile Early Phonics activities • Toe-by-Toe • Specific 1–1 teaching to targets • Time out lunchtime support • Phonics group • 1–1 reading • Precision teaching • Phonological Awareness training (PAT) • Listen and Do tapes • Individualised behaviour programme • Lunchtime Activity room • SENCO assessment	• Speech & Language Therapy 1–1/group work • LEA SEN support service observation and advice/ input to IEPs • LEA SEN support service groupwork • LEA SEN support service Phono-graphix 1–1 • Revolving door project with local special school – short-term placements for children with SEBD • LEA SEN support service Social Skills group • LEA SEN support service Circle of friends • LEA SEN support service Anger Management 1–1/ group • Pastoral Support planning/action • LEA Primary Inclusion Team • Mental health nurse counselling • Attendance worker

Table 6.5c Primary school SEN provision map 2002–2003 Years 5 and 6

Year	In-class specific differentiation strategies	School Action	School Action Plus
Year 5/6	Enhanced LSA support for : • Regular group teaching lit/num • Easy Learn worksheets • Lit/num games from SEN base • Paired reading • Abacus Maths activities • Charles Cripps 'A Hand for Spelling' • Group topic mats • Group literacy mats • Group numeracy mats • Springboard maths • Further Literacy Support (FLS)	• Small group teaching lit/numeracy, using, e.g. Word shark (ICT), Number Shark (ICT) Eye for Spelling (ICT), Wizards Spelling programme, Stile Spelling Programme, modified ALS & FLS and Springboard • Specific 1–1 teaching to targets • Time out lunchtime support • Phonics group • 1–1 reading • Toe-by-Toe • Precision teaching • Phonological Awareness training (PAT) • Individualised behaviour programme • Programme Achieve (self-esteem) • Lunchtime Activity room • SENCO assessment • LSA Language group	• Speech & Language Therapy 1–1/group work • LEA SEN support service observation and advice/input to IEPs • LEA SEN support service groupwork • LEA SEN support service Phono-graphix 1–1 • Revolving door project with local special school – short term placements for children with SEBD • LEA SEN support service Social Skills group • LEA SEN support service Circle of Friends • LEA SEN support service Anger Management 1–1/group • Pastoral Support planning/action • LEA Primary Inclusion Team • Mental health nurse counselling • Attendance worker

Table 6.6 Matching action to levels of special educational need

Level of need	Assessment and planning	Grouping for teaching purposes	Human resources	Curriculum and teaching methods
Lower threshold of need Class-based differentiation	Part of normal school and class assessments. SENCO may be involved in informal/formalised assessment to inform future planning. Normal curriculum planning showing specific differentiation for groups of children. May have group targets within curriculum plans. Concerns discussed with parents.	Pupil based in ordinary classroom. Grouping strategies used flexibly within the classroom.	Main provision by class teacher. LSA support used routinely. SENCO may be involved in informal/formal assessment. Outside agencies might offer observations relating to whole class strategies.	Emphasis on differentiation for curriculum access. Possibly some specific reinforcement or skill development activities in support of group targets.
Increased level of need School Action	Use of more specific assessment or observation which might involve outside agencies' advice. Planning to include individually focused IEPs though this could still involve some group targets. Parents involved regularly and support targets at home. Pupils involved in setting and monitoring their targets.	Pupil based in ordinary classroom plus regular opportunities for adult supported groupwork. There may be opportunities for some individual support of specific IEP targets in or out of class.	Main provision by class teacher. Pupil support is used routinely in the classroom, with some targeted support provided by LSA to group or 1–1. SENCO may be involved in working with groups or individuals.	Emphasis placed on increased differentiation of activities, language use and materials. Some use of specific programmes and/or materials to support individual targets.
Higher threshold of need School Action Plus	Involvement of education and non-education professionals in assessment and planning. All IEP targets are individualised, short-term and specific. Parents and pupils (as appropriate) involved in all target setting and review.	Pupil works predominantly in small groups with an adult in and out of class. Opportunities for some 1–1 support focused on specific IEP targets.	Pupil support used routinely in the ordinary classroom with sustained targeted support provided by LSA on individual/group basis to include withdrawal. Specialist teacher and/or SENCO may be involved.	Increasingly individualized programme within an inclusive curriculum. Use of specific programmes and/or materials.

go towards meeting special needs provision. This might include any of the following:

- any proportion of the Age-Weighted Pupil Unit which local policies allocate to SEN;
- any funding to meet additional educational needs based on a formula (such as the proportion of children eligible for free school meals, or prior attainment);
- any funding based on an LEA audit of children with SEN in the school;
- any delegated funding for Statements of SEN;
- any delegated funding for the purchase of support at School Action Plus;
- any Standards Fund allocations specifically linked to SEN.

We looked closely at our provision and drew out what was needed by way of human or physical resources to maintain it, in each year group. Where staffing was required it was then necessary to translate staff involvement/roles into time, and from that work out what this would cost. It is important that you include on-costs (school contributions towards pensions and national insurance). LEAs provide head teachers with ready reckoners for this, and they are invaluable in carrying out this activity.

When costing your provision you need to consider:

- learning support assistant or nursery nurse costs (calculate this as an average if you have a number to calculate for);
- SEN teacher costs;
- SENCO costs: the Code of Practice makes clear that the basic costs of the SENCO (salary increments and some time for the coordination role) have to come from the school's general base budget, but if the SENCO does direct SEN teaching or EBD support with individuals or groups of children, this would come from SEN funding;
- any additional lunchtime supervisor provision which is targeted, for example, at meeting the needs of children with social, emotional and behavioural difficulties;
- any provision at School Action Plus which you have to purchase, using the school's SEN budget;
- any costs of additional space, for example if you rent a room elsewhere for specific provision such as counselling, physiotherapy, or a nurture group;
- maintenance of small sets or support classes, where this is specifically intended to raise the achievement of pupils with SEN. You can calculate the additional cost of having a very small class like this: calculate the cost of an average-sized class (between 26 and 35 pupils) by dividing the average hourly cost of a teacher by the number of pupils in the class. This gives the cost per child in the average-sized class. Do the same again but divide by the number of pupils in the smaller class. This gives the average cost per child in the support class. Take away the cost per pupil in the average class. This sum is the per pupil cost of the SEN support;

- the costs of resources and equipment, including insurance, maintenance and repair.

You might also include some head teacher or deputy head teacher time within your costs, if within their role they have specific SEN time built in. This time should be time which is *planned*, however, rather than time which is reactive or disciplinary.

Your SEN provision map should only include provision which is additional to, or different from, that available to all pupils. For example, you would include a lunchtime club designed for pupils with behaviour problems, but you would not include lunchtime library sessions that are open to all pupils.

Having set costs against provision you have a clear indication of the way budgets have been allocated. It may be that you have over or under spent. It will further help you with planning strategically for SEN, as when you are evaluating outcomes against support and action you will have a clearer picture of the 'value for money' your SEN provision provides.

7 Planning provision: what works?

Introduction

In Chapter 6 we looked at how to plan provision for children with SEN on the basis of audited needs and available funding. There is, however, a third piece to the provision mapping jigsaw: information on which types of provision are likely to be effective – information on 'what works'.

In this chapter we will try to complete the jigsaw by evaluating the evidence for a range of different

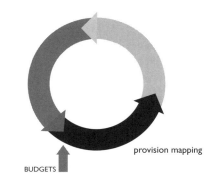

Figure 7.1 The school improvement cycle

types of provision in which strategic managers might choose to invest their available funding in order to meet the identified needs.

We will look at this evidence under a number of headings: from early intervention to provision for literacy and mathematical difficulties, and for disaffection and emotional/behavioural difficulties. First, however, we will look at the evidence on the effectiveness of the provision choices currently made very widely in schools.

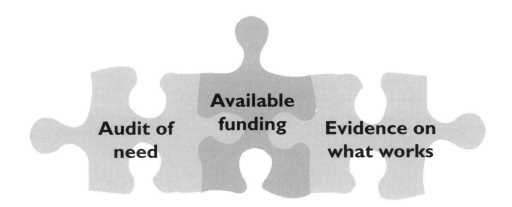

Current choices

Teaching assistant support

> Schools now have full control over their budget for special needs provision. They can spend it how they like. They can choose to buy in staff from the ex-LEA support service for advice, training, assessment, teaching – or not. They can cast the net wider for someone to provide any or all of these services, or they can get in Mrs Bloggs from down the road who knows the school and is willing to 'do small groups' twice a week.
>
> (Editorial, *Special Children*, April 2002)

On the whole, the evidence suggests that it is the 'Mrs Bloggs' option which the majority of head teachers choose when planning their SEN provision.

A recent survey of head teachers (Archer *et al.* 2002), for example, found that SEN was a main area of concern for many of them: 43 per cent saw this as a priority. In this context, when asked how they would spend a hypothetical 5 per cent increase in their school budget, 78 per cent chose classroom/welfare assistants as their top priority. Actual figures for growth in support staff numbers confirm these expressed preferences: between 2001 and 2002 the numbers of SEN support assistants rose by 24 per cent, and stands currently at almost double the 1998 total (Howson 2002).

Many individual teaching assistants are outstandingly effective; no one who has worked with children with SEN can doubt this. Overall, however, there is a lack of evidence about the impact of additional teaching assistant support on raising pupils' attainment or promoting inclusion. Sometimes it seems that the presence of a teaching assistant effectively prevents the child from interacting with his or her peers (MENCAP 1999; Farrell *et al.* 1999).

Often, it prevents the class teacher from considering their own role in adapting the curriculum to ensure their pupils' access and participation (Derington *et al.* 1996; Lorenz 1999; Tennant 2001).

In relation to raising attainment, longitudinal research has failed to find statistical evidence showing that the number of teaching assistants/additional adults in the classroom has an influence on children's educational progress (Blatchford *et al.* 2002). On the other hand, while noting that there are pupils with SEN who are now spending more time than they should with teaching assistants rather than with teachers, HMI (Ofsted 2002: 5) found that the presence of teaching assistants can improve the quality of teaching, particularly 'where the teaching assistant is following a prescribed intervention or catch-up programme, for which they had received training, and worked in close partnership with the teacher'.

What does not seem to be effective, in relation to inclusion or to raising attainment, is the diffuse, unfocused 'support' through which an additional adult is attached to an individual child, as if by Velcro, with no clear objectives for their work, and little training or management support.

The key issue for managers, then, in planning their SEN provision, is not so much whether to invest in additional adult time, but to make strategic choices about what exactly it is that the additional adults will be doing – what prescribed intervention they will be using. It is here that available knowledge on the impact of different types of intervention, to which we will return later in this chapter, will be useful.

Reducing class sizes

Another choice frequently made by managers in their SEN spending is to reduce class sizes across the school, or selectively for certain year groups or for lower sets. Intuitively, most teachers feel sure that smaller class sizes must lead to improved pupil outcomes, because of the increased amount of attention they are able to give to each child. Since children with SEN are felt to need even more individual support and attention than other children, smaller class sizes must, the argument goes, benefit them even more than their peers.

The research evidence on the link between smaller class sizes and pupil achievement, however, on the whole runs counter to teachers' and managers' intuition. Several major reviews of the international research literature (Hanushek 1997; Bennett 1998; Blatchford and Mortimore 1994) have failed to find that smaller classes lead to improved pupil achievement overall. The only exception is in the early years, particularly for socially disadvantaged children, where class size is reduced below 15 children: here, the Tennessee 'STAR' project (Krueger 1999) did find that when children aged 5 to 8 were randomly allocated to large (22 to 24 pupil) and small (14 to 16 pupil) classes, children in smaller classes did significantly better. The benefits were greater for children from minority ethnic groups and for children from poorer backgrounds. More recently, an important UK study (Blatchford *et al.* 2002) investigated the educational effects of class size difference and adult:pupil ratios in Reception and Key Stage 1 classes in nine LEAs. This study found significant effects for class sizes in the Reception year on children's progress in literacy and mathematics. In literacy, though not in maths, children who started out as low achievers at school entry showed the greatest benefits. In Year 1 and Year 2, however, there was no clear statistical evidence of an effect of class size. Increasing the ratio of adults to pupils through the provision of additional adult support from teaching assistants or others had no effect on children's attainment in any of the three year groups studied.

A number of different explanations have been proffered for the counter-intuitive findings on class size. The most convincing is that reducing class size, of itself, does not change teacher behaviour – unless the class becomes sufficiently small for the teacher to be able to plan for and respond to each child as an individual, rather than as one of a small group.

For school managers adopting a strategic approach to SEN, the implications are that they should think very carefully before investing school funding for additional or special educational needs into marginal reductions in class size, particularly in Key Stages 2, 3 and 4. Such measures may reduce stress on teachers, but despite this are very unlikely to produce a return on the investment in the form of improved pupil outcomes.

Setting

Another popular strategy adopted by managers to raise attainment is setting pupils by ability. Use of setting has grown in recent years (Sukhnandan and Lee 1998). Again, however, there is very little evidence that setting improves attainment.

While an early Ofsted report (Ofsted 1999a) found that the use of setting in primary schools led to impressive gains in national tests in setted subjects, more recent reports have been more cautious. Ofsted's recent reports on the implementation of the National Numeracy Strategy, for example, have noted that there were fewer examples of very good teaching in lower sets and no overall trend for the quality of teaching to be better in setted classes.

A study carried out by the National Institute of Economic and Social Research (Whitburn 2001) of the progress of 1,200 children at Key Stage 2 found that the test results of mixed-ability classes were up to 7 per cent higher than those achieved in sets. Mixed-ability classes were of particular benefit to slower learners, while levels of attainment in more able children did not suffer.

Several studies have found that setting in secondary schools is equally ineffective. Hallam (1996), for example, reviewed the international research literature from 1919 to 2001 and found that setting made no difference to pupil attainment overall in English and had a negative impact on the progress of lower ability pupils in Maths. Able pupils, however, did do better in schools which used setting. Harlen and Malcolm (1999) reviewed research and concluded that 'there is no consistent and reliable evidence of positive effects of setting and streaming in any subjects or for pupils of particular ability levels'. Sukhnandan and Lee (1998) reached the same conclusion for pupils at both primary and secondary levels, across all subject areas and despite pupils' levels of ability (high, middle or low). Sukhnandan and Lee also noted the detrimental effect of setting on the attitudes and self-esteem of pupils of lower ability. Low-ability pupils placed in sets, compared to low-ability pupils taught in mixed-ability classes, were also less likely to participate in school activities, experienced more disciplinary problems, and had a higher level of absenteeism.

Finally, many researchers have shown that low-ability sets tend to contain a disproportionately large number of boys, socially disadvantaged pupils, pupils from minority ethnic backgrounds and summer-born children. In this respect, setting serves to reinforce existing social divisions and lead to a 'vicious circle of underachievement from which it is difficult for these pupils to escape' (Sukhnandan and Lee 1998).

There are, of course, always individual exceptions to the general picture that emerges from large-scale research. Where a lower set is allocated an exceptionally skilled teacher, who is able to avoid the tendency to hold low and self-fulfilling expectations of what children can achieve, and where the school monitors the composition of lower sets carefully, and the impact on pupil self-esteem equally carefully, it may well be possible to use smaller sets effectively as an SEN intervention.

Unless they are sure that these conditions can be in place, however, strategic managers are unlikely – in the face of the evidence – to choose setting as a value for money investment. There is little evidence that it will contribute to raising attainment, promoting inclusion or improving the behaviour of children with difficulties with learning.

Alternative choices

Early intervention programmes

Few teachers, head teachers or SENCOs need any convincing of the value of intervening *early* when children are at risk of experiencing difficulties in learning or in social, emotional and behavioural development. Common sense alone dictates that intervention is more likely to be successful if put in place before the point where any early difficulties have become compounded by the social and emotional effects of failure to learn or relate well to others: low self-esteem, peer rejection, frustration, anger or despondency.

There is, moreover, a good deal of evidence which backs up this common-sense view. A number of influential reviews of the literature (e.g. Brooks-Gunn 2001; Campbell and Ramey 1994) have documented the long-term positive outcomes for children's achievement and social adjustment of certain kinds of intervention in the early years. An equal number of studies depressingly document the long-term consequences if young children's difficulties are left unaddressed: that over 40 per cent of seven- and eight-year-olds with 'conduct disorders' (i.e., challenging behaviour) go on to a pattern of habitual delinquency in adolescence, that unaddressed severe literacy difficulties link closely with later experience of exclusion from school and that some 50–60 per cent of the prison population also show evidence of difficulties in acquiring literacy skills.

The case for early intervention is clear. The way in which the special educational needs system is currently implemented in the majority of schools and LEAs, however, militates against early intervention. The SEN Code of Practice itself is designed around the principle of applying the minimum possible help and support for children at an early stage, and increasing this by small incremental steps if children continue to struggle. Intervention that is substantial (in terms of cost and level of expertise of those involved) inevitably comes late on in this process. In order to manage constantly escalating budget pressures, most LEA funding systems require evidence of several years of lack of progress, despite action taken at school level, before substantial funding is put in place.

Where it is put in place, it is almost always at the individual child level, and if it involves a Statement, it may 'arrive' at any point in the school year, thus precluding any kind of cost-effective pre-planned intervention.

The trend towards greater delegation of SEN funding to school level, however, is beginning to open up the possibility that imaginative school managers can pre-empt the pattern of funding following, rather than preventing, repeated failure. Many schools will, increasingly, be able to choose to invest their SEN funding differently in the early years of schooling.

If schools do this, what information is available to guide them on the forms of provision which are likely to be effective? Some answers can be found in a very helpful publication, *Intervening Early*, from the DfES and Coram Family (2002). This publication focuses on children's social, emotional and behavioural development. It first recommends whole-school approaches that are likely to reduce the overall numbers of children requiring additional help with their social adjustment or behaviour. On the basis of hard evidence of effectiveness, it recommends the use of Jenny Mosley's Whole School Quality Circle Time model (Mosley 1993), a PSHE programme called the Nurturing Programme offered by the voluntary organisation Family Links (Barlow and Stewart-Brown 1999) and You Can Do It! – another PSHE programme which focuses on raising achievement as well as on social goals (Barnard 2000).

It then goes on to review a number of small-group interventions which have been shown to have powerful, long-term, positive effects on children who have been identified early on as requiring additional help. Three 'programs' are particularly recommended: nurture groups; structured group work on social skills, combined with parenting groups; and a programme specifically designed for vulnerable and withdrawn children in their early years of school.

Nurture groups

Nurture Groups are very small classes (typically 10–12 pupils), set up in Key Stage 1 for children who have not developed in their early years the social, linguistic and cognitive skills they need in order to learn. The classes, run by a teacher and a teaching assistant, provide children with structured experiences which fill in gaps caused by early disrupted parenting, social deprivation or unmet emotional needs. They are targeted at problems which are assumed to stem 'from the erosion of early care and support in families suffering severe fragmentation and stress' (Bennathan and Boxall 2000). Children in the groups will be those who are seriously disruptive or withdrawn and who are unable to settle, listen, concentrate, share or make friends. They come to feel secure within their predictable daily routines and trusting relationships with reliable adults. They learn basic skills of managing in a group: listening, taking turns, waiting, following a task through, making choices and cooperating with others.

At the beginning, nurture groups were generally full-time, with children staying in the group for between two and four terms, then gradually reintegrating into a regular-sized class. More recently, some schools have developed models based on part-time attendance.

The nurture group model is not cheap. A school implementing a nurture group needs to invest in staffing sufficient to bring the normal Key Stage 1 class size of 25–30 down to 12 in one group. It needs to provide an additional classroom, and fund initial staff training for the teacher and teaching assistant involved.

The research on nurture groups, however, suggests this investment substantially reduces the cost of supporting, over the longer term, children who have not had this early intervention experience. In the London Borough of Enfield, where nurture groups were first introduced, the progress of children who had been in nurture groups was compared with that of a control group of children who had similar needs but had not taken part in a group (Iszatt and Wasilewska 1997). The study showed that three times as many children in the control group later required a Statement for special educational provision than those who had been in nurture groups. The proportion of children who went on to EBD Special School was almost seven times higher in the control group. Work on costings (Bennathan and Boxall 2000) showed that a primary school might have to spend four times as much later on in supporting a child who had needed but had not had access to nurture group provision than they would by placing the child in a nurture group in the early years of schooling.

Gains are not only evident in children's emotional and social development. Recent research at Cambridge University found measured improvements in speech and language skills, and baseline assessment. The Cambridge study of 342 children who attended nurture groups has also found further evidence of the impact on emotional and behavioural difficulties. At entry to the nurture group programme, 92 per cent of the children were in the abnormal or borderline range on a standardised questionnaire measuring social, emotional and behavioural difficulties, compared to 85 per cent of a matched control group attending mainstream classes. After two terms in the nurture group this changed to 64 per cent for the children who had been in the group, compared to 75 per cent for the control group.

Schools may also want to consider the cost-effectiveness of nurture groups in terms of their effect on other children and staff: as one school governor, enthusiastic about the benefits of the nurture group provision in her school, put it: 'One troubled child can affect the life of the whole school' (DfES and Coram Family 2002: 33).

(Details of where to find out more about nurture groups, along with other intervention programmes described in this chapter, can be found in the further information section at the end of this book.)

Social skills group work and parenting support

Another highly effective form of early intervention is structured, time-limited social skills group work for children at risk of developing long-term social, emotional and behavioural difficulty – ideally combined with support for the difficult task of parenting.

Such groups work best when rooted in whole-school approaches to developing children's skills in understanding their own and others' feelings, and solving social problems, such as those described earlier in this chapter. As with any teaching, what is learned in any form of additional intervention outside the classroom needs to be linked closely to what goes on every day within the classroom and – in the case of social and emotional learning – in the playground, dining-hall and corridors as well.

One particularly effective programme is that devised by Carolyn Webster-Stratton, which has been widely evaluated in the USA and increasingly in this country also. The programme is aimed at four- to eight-year-olds with conduct problems which may include aggression, defiance, poor concentration and hyperactivity, and difficulty in making friends.

The programme, 'Dinosaur School', uses puppets and video to model positive social skills, which children then discuss, apply and practise. The programme typically lasts between three and six months; children attend the group weekly for about two-and-a-half hours. Group leaders (one or two, depending upon the size of the group) must be specially trained; sometimes they are health professionals and sometimes teachers with specialist EBD expertise.

Children who have taken part in a Dinosaur School group demonstrate significantly less aggression than control groups with similar needs who have not taken part in a group. They develop strategies to manage conflict and relate positively to others. Follow-up assessment indicates that the improvements are maintained over time (Webster-Stratton *et al.* 2001).

On its own, then, group work of this kind has a significant and lasting impact. When group work with children is combined with parent support groups, however, the effects become even stronger: whereas 75 per cent of children show improvements a year after they have been in a group, 95 per cent show improvements where their families have also been involved in the programme (Webster-Stratton and Hammond 1997).

Family support, in the Webster-Stratton programme, takes the form of courses run once a week by trained workers alongside the work with the children. Courses use video and involve demonstration, discussion and 'home practice' in a range of skills, from responding to children in shared play through to setting limits, being consistent and using positive reinforcement. The group is an important part of the process; group members get to know one another well and provide mutual support during the programme and after it ends.

The Webster-Stratton programme is among many effective parent support programmes which may be available locally for schools to tap into. What successful parenting programmes seem to share (Barlow 1999) are the following characteristics:

- They will involve groups rather than working with parents on an individual basis.
- They will be community-based (taking place in local settings which are readily accessible and where parents feel at ease) rather than clinic-based.
- They will make at least some use of 'behavioural techniques' within a structured programme.

Schools are rarely in a position to organise parent support groups on their own. In partnership with educational psychologists, LEA EBD support teams and health staff, including school nurses and clinical psychologists, however, they are in a powerful position to host, and sometimes part-fund, the kind of combined parent–child interventions which have been shown to be effective. A limited investment in work of this kind early on is likely to prove very much more cost-effective than having to allocate learning support assistants to children later on in order to contain behaviour that has become entrenched and increasingly difficult to manage.

Children who are vulnerable and withdrawn

While social skills groups tend to focus on children who 'act out' inner disturbance through defiance, aggression and challenge, there is another group of children for whom early intervention can have profound positive effects. These are children who demonstrate their troubled emotions by withdrawing into themselves and becoming isolated, hard to reach and low in self-esteem.

National Pyramid Trust clubs are targeted at children like these, in the 7–9 age group. After a screening process which involves class teachers and outside agencies, children are offered the chance to join after-school clubs, running one day a week for ten weeks. The clubs are staffed and run by volunteers, whom the Pyramid Trust recruit and train. The volunteers plan activities which will help the groups to bond, and which will enable all children to experience a sense of success and belonging.

The groups are highly cost-effective. Schools contribute a small amount, and commit time for a link teacher to liaise with those directly involved in running the clubs. Research has shown that nearly 60 per cent of children who attend show improved self-esteem, compared with 25 per cent in a control group. Improvements in attendance, relationships with peers and academic skills have also been reported (Makins 1997; Skinner 1996).

Early language and literacy skills

So far, the early interventions we have looked at have focused primarily on children's social and emotional development. Many teachers will recognise this as an appropriate focus: as they well know, if young children are not able to concentrate, cooperate and respond to adults and peers, these areas must be tackled before they are ready to learn.

Schools which take a strategic approach to SEN and want their provision to make a real difference will, however, also want to invest in early intervention to tackle language and literacy difficulties.

There is increasing concern among head teachers (McLelland 2002) that children now come into school with immature and under-developed spoken language skills. There is also concrete evidence (Locke *et al.* 2002) that more than half of all children who live in areas of high social deprivation may have significant language delay.

Early language difficulties tend to have long-term consequences. In one study (Sheridan and Peckham 1975) over half of children identified as having language problems at age 7 demonstrated residual language problems and learning, social or emotional difficulties at 16; difficulties in reading are particularly likely (Aram and Nation 1980; Gallagher *et al.* 2000).

What can be done to prevent these long-term consequences? Interventions with school-age children have not been widely researched, in contrast to the extensive work done on intervention within the home and in pre-school settings. Nevertheless, there is evidence that it is possible to make a significant difference through school-based programmes.

One successful programme is Talking Partners. Originating in Bradford, Talking Partners is a short-term intervention delivered in Reception/Year 1 by a trained helper (teaching assistant or volunteer) over a period of ten weeks. The programme consists of three 20-minute sessions per week of structured activities to promote oral language development. It is closely aligned with the National Literacy Strategy (with many activities linked to texts) and can be delivered within the Literacy Hour.

Data from the initial implementation of the programme in Years 1 to 3 show gains on average of 13 to 18 months on standardised tests of expressive language (Hilditch 2002).

Another programme with evidence of impact is Teaching Talking (Locke and Beech 1991). This is a commercially available package which provides a structured process for school-based diagnostic assessment, intervention and monitoring for children with language difficulties. Its use in one Education Action Zone (Dann 2002) reduced the percentage of Reception children with below-age language skills from 27 per cent to 6 per cent over a period of nine months.

Early language intervention is, of itself, likely to reduce the numbers of children requiring additional support with literacy – the most commonly identified area of SEN in all schools, and the area where provision needs to be particularly carefully chosen and targeted if schools' SEN spending is to have a significant impact on outcomes.

Provision for literacy difficulties in children of all ages is covered in detail later in this chapter. With respect to early intervention, there are a number of programmes which have a strong evidence base. Reading Recovery, for example, works with the very lowest attainers in Year 1 (and sometimes Year 2) and has proved itself successful, internationally and in the UK, in returning approximately 80 per cent of these children to average levels of literacy for their class. Follow-up to the end of Key Stage 1 SATs shows (Reading Recovery National Network 2001) that 66 per cent of the 3,000 children receiving the programme in England and Wales in 2000–2001 achieved level 2 or above in reading, and 67 per cent in writing.

The costs for the school of implementing Reading Recovery can appear high, as it involves employing at least a half-time teacher who works one-to-one for half an hour a day with each child supported, for a period of 12 to 20 weeks. The cost per child, however (given that the intervention is for a short period only, and that the effects are so long-lasting), is, again, very much less than the amount spent in the long term on supporting the child whose literacy difficulties persist throughout their schooling. Hurry and Sylva (1998) suggest that though Reading Recovery is expensive at the point of delivery, averaged out over a five-year period the cost of supporting Reading Recovery children was only 10 per cent more than the cost of learning support which schools usually provide, as calculated from 'control' (non-Reading Recovery) schools in their study.

Reading Recovery is one of the very few early intervention programmes whose impact has been followed up long-term. Some international investigators find positive evidence for lasting improvements (Moore and

Wade 1998; Pinnell *et al.* 1994). Research in Australia and New Zealand (Moore and Wade 1998) followed up children who had experienced Reading Recovery at age 6, when they were between 10 and 12 years of age, and found them still significantly ahead of a comparison group who had not had Reading Recovery, in reading accuracy and comprehension, in attitudes to reading and in length and quality of writing. Other researchers, however, find that gains are not always sustained (Chapman *et al.* 1998).

In the UK, Hurry and Sylva (1998) found that 70 per cent of children who had received Reading Recovery at age 6 were still within the average band of their class four years later. Children eligible for free school meals and those who were non-readers when they began Reading Recovery at 6, showed the greatest long-term benefits.

Another early intervention with a strong record in Key Stage 1 is the Better Reading Partnership. The Better Reading Partnership is based on principles similar to those of Reading Recovery; instead of using teachers who have a full year's on-the-job training, however, it uses a range of adults such as teaching assistants and volunteers, who receive a two-day training course and ongoing monitoring and support. The adults, or 'partners', then read together with pupils three times a week, for approximately 15 minutes, one to one. The evidence (Brooks 2002) suggests that children make rapid progress over the period of intervention.

Family Literacy is a programme devised by the Basic Skills Agency. It is based on the evidence that children are more likely to experience difficulties if their parents also have weak literacy skills. The programme aims to break this cycle of deprivation by working with parents to improve their literacy skills at the same time as it works with their children. Its goal is to ensure that they feel more confident in their ability to help their children in the future. The course is intensive: eight hours a week for 12 weeks, in two separate sessions. Evaluations (Brooks 2002) show substantial gains for the children involved, sustained at follow-up several years later.

Provision for children with literacy difficulties

Given the national statistics that, currently, around 7 per cent of children leave primary school operating at below level 3 in English (i.e., with literacy skills no greater than the level of the average seven- or eight-year-old) and that 11 per cent are below level 4 at the end of Key Stage 3, and that there has been no change in these percentages over the past few years, despite an ever-increasing national spend on SEN, there is an urgent need for schools to review the provision they make for children who experience literacy difficulties.

A multitude of programmes and schemes are available, all purporting to tackle literacy difficulties and produce long-lasting gains. The evidence on the efficacy of these programmes has been reviewed in a recent report commissioned by the National Literacy Strategy (Brooks 2002). The review draws out some general principles:

- Work on phonological skills can be very effective, but needs to make the links between the phonological learning and application to texts.
- It is possible to improve children's comprehension by using schemes targeted specifically at this area.
- Working on children's self-esteem together with their reading has proved very successful.
- Many much-touted ICT-based Individual Learning Systems (ILS) have not proved their worth; smaller-scale applications of ICT (such as using talking word processors to support work on phonics) have, however, demonstrated good results.
- Schemes which initially appear costly in terms of the involvement of teachers rather than teaching assistants, and substantial amounts of training, can give good value for money in the longer term. Children with the most severe literacy difficulties may only be able to catch up if they receive skilled support of this kind.
- Where reading partners (volunteer adults, peers or parents/carers) are available and can be given appropriate training and support, partnership approaches to such paired reading can be very effective for children with less severe difficulties.
- Short, focused interventions lasting 12–20 weeks can have good impact; interventions lasting longer than this do not necessarily produce proportionally greater benefits.

The review covered all the main schemes and programmes reported by LEAs to be in use in their schools; it reports on 29 specific schemes for which it was possible to obtain some evidence of evaluation. Where a scheme was not included, this was because evaluation evidence was lacking.

The 29 schemes were compared in terms of their immediate impact on reading attainment. One measure used was ratio gain: the amount of progress in reading and spelling age, in months, divided by the time in months during which the gains were made. A ratio gain of one (one month's gain in one month of tuition) would equate to the normal average progress made by all children in the population as a whole. For children who are behind in literacy, ratio gains need to be higher than one if they are to begin to catch up with their peers.

Particularly effective schemes, in terms of ratio gains, were, for reading accuracy:

- Acceleread, Accelewrite
- Phono-graphix™
- The Catch Up Project (in some implementations though not others)
- Better Reading Partnership in Year 1 to Year 6
- Multisensory teaching system for reading (MTSR)
- Reciprocal Teaching
- THRASS
- Paired reading.

Table 7.1 Literacy programmes

Scheme	Age group	Delivered by	Description
Acceleread, Accelewrite	Years 3 to 9	Supervising TA	TA works with individual child for 20 mins a day for 4 weeks using talking word processor to type sentences following phonic patterns
Phono-graphix	Key Stages 1–4	Teacher plus TA or parent	The teacher works with the child 1-1 for one hour per week, supplemented by 3x20 min sessions with TA or parent for 12–26 weeks. Phonics-based plus practice in reading texts of own choice
Catch-up project	Key Stages 2 and 3	Teacher	10–15 minute individual session once or twice a week for approx. 10 months, involving reading a text and a linked writing or spelling activity
Better Reading Partnership	Key Stages 1 and 2	Volunteer adult or TA	The adult reads 1–1 with the child three times a week for approx. 15 mins over a 10-week period
Multi-sensory teaching system for reading (MTSR)	Key Stages 1 and 2	Teacher	A scripted, multi-sensory package for teaching word level reading, used with groups of children for 20 mins a day, four days a week, over a period of approx. 12–20 weeks
Reciprocal teaching	Key Stages 2 to 4	Teacher	The teacher works with a group, modelling text comprehension strategies; pupils are gradually encouraged to take on the role of the teacher
THRASS	Key Stages 1 to 4	Teacher	A structured multi-sensory word-level programme covering handwriting, reading and spelling; individual or group.
Paired reading	All ages	Parent, volunteer or another pupil	A simple technique used to practice reading aloud, first supported and then alone. Varying durations.
Cued spelling	All ages	Parent, volunteer or another pupil	Paired work in spelling based on choosing cues to remember a word – 3 x 15 mins a week for approx. 16 weeks.

A brief description of each of these programmes and its target group is provided in Table 7.1. Details of how to find out more about the programmes can be found in the further information section at the end of this book.

Measures of reading comprehension were used less frequently than measures of reading accuracy (such as the number of single words from a list read correctly). Where they were used, the following schemes proved effective:

- Inference training
- Phono-graphix™

- Paired reading
- THRASS
- Reciprocal teaching

All of these schemes achieved, at least in the short term, ratio gains for reading accuracy and comprehension of at least two (doubling the normal rate of progress); with some schemes children made eight times the normal rate of progress.

The implications for schools' strategic choices are clear: if your own evaluation shows that children with literacy difficulties are not, on average, making at least two months' progress per month of intervention or 'support', you will want to reconsider the type of provision you are making.

You may want to bear in mind, when choosing alternative provision, that only some of the successful interventions have been followed up over time to check whether the programme had a lasting impact. The schemes from the 'best buy' lists above which have positive follow-up evidence over a follow-up period of up to one year are Acceleread, Accelewrite, Paired Reading and Better Reading Partnership. Only Reading Recovery and Family Literacy have been systematically followed up over a longer period (three to four years), with evidence that at least some of the gains are maintained, as discussed in the early intervention section in this chapter.

So far we have looked at the impact of particular types of provision on reading. Writing and spelling have received less attention in the literature. Greg Brooks' study does, however, point to Acceleread Accelewrite, Cued Spelling and Phono-graphix™ as consistently effective, with MTSR and THRASS effective in some studies and some age groups, but not all.

Writing composition, as distinct from transcription (spelling and handwriting), has been researched least of all. We do know, however, that Reading Recovery has a long-term positive impact on the rate and quantity of children's writing (on a rating scale) and the amount that they write (Moore and Wade 1998).

Family Literacy also seems to impact on the quality of writing, as does a scheme called Paired Writing (Sutherland and Topping 1999), in which pairs of children use a multi-step structure (ideas – drafting – editing) which scaffolds collaborative writing.

Provision for children with difficulties in mathematics

Nearly as many children have difficulty with mathematics as with literacy: 5 per cent leave primary schools below level 3, and 11 per cent are below level 4 at the end of Key Stage 3. There is a dearth of evaluation information, however, on specific programmes which help them make progress.

Most of the programmes which have been researched focus on early intervention in Key Stage 1. Mathematics Recovery, for example, is a one-to-one, intensive (daily) teaching system for children in Year 1, based on detailed diagnostic assessment. Evaluations in Australia, the USA and the UK have shown that children make significant progress, many of them catching up with their peers (Wright, Martland and Stafford 2000).

Mathematics Recovery is a well-established scheme, with training and materials available in this country from staff at the University of Liverpool. A newer scheme, which has so far only been piloted but which looks promising, is Numeracy Recovery. This programme works with six- and seven-year-olds and is less intense than Mathematics Recovery, involving only half an hour of intervention per week for approximately 30 weeks. Dowker (2001) presents evidence of outcomes for 122 children which shows significant gains on standardised tests of numerical operations, with the improvements maintained a year later.

In areas of social deprivation, Family Numeracy, a programme which works with groups of children and their parents, appears to be as successful as its Family Literacy counterpart in raising attainment and breaking a cycle of familial under-achievement.

All three programmes involve additional time from adults. Where this is not possible, Paired Maths (another off-shoot from literacy programmes – in this case Paired Reading and Paired Spelling) offers an alternative, involving pairs of children working together on a tutoring programme which, again, has been shown to have a significant impact, in a series of well-designed research studies (Topping and Ehly 1998).

Interventions to raise overall attainment and improve academic engagement

Peer tutoring

There is a good deal of evidence to show that peer tutoring – where one child (either from the same class or an older age group) takes on a direct teaching role with another – can be a highly effective intervention for children experiencing difficulties in learning. One study (Levin and Glass 1986), for example, compared the effect of an increase in teaching time, a reduction in class size, computer-assisted learning and peer tutoring, and found that only the latter was effective in raising attainment.

Peer tutoring is effective in many curriculum areas: mathematics, spelling, language development, ICT skills and problem solving (Charlton 1998; Topping and Ehly 1998).

This may be, in part, because teaching a new concept or skill to another person helps to deepen and consolidate the tutor's own learning, and in part because taking on a responsible role in helping another child increases self-esteem.

This latter effect has made it a useful strategy for tackling disaffection: as in, for example, the Valued Youth Programme which operates in Birmingham, Greenwich and Hammersmith & Fulham. In this programme, secondary-age students at risk of educational failure tutor younger students. Evaluation (Davies 2000) has shown that the programme achieved its aim in terms of promoting tutors' self-confidence and willingness to attend school. School staff described improvement in the young people's self-esteem, communication and organisational skills, although not in their behaviour or attitudes in class.

Maher (1984) reports several highly successful projects in which 14–16-year-olds with a history of disruptive behaviour and underachievement tutored 9–11-year-old slow learners over a period of ten weeks. The older pupils showed massive gains in school attendance and performance; the tutees showed improvement of 15–20 per cent in task completion and performance on attainment tests. While cross-age tutoring has particular benefits for improving tutors' engagement with learning, same-age tutoring also works very well. There have been many reports, for example, of successful schemes that have divided classes or year groups into two on the basis of reading ability and established reading partnerships involving every child (Horner 1990; Leeves 1990).

Peer tutoring is an inexpensive resource, but not one without cost. Research has shown that if it is to be effective, teachers or other adults need to invest time in providing training for the tutors and in ongoing monitoring and support of the project while it is underway.

Study support and out-of-hours learning

This section covers a range of study support programmes including breakfast clubs, after-school clubs and summer schools. Schemes such as these have been promoted by the DfES, on the basis of evidence of the success of after-school enrichment programmes and holiday schemes in the USA, particularly in areas of social deprivation.

There is some UK evidence in their favour. A major research project conducted by NFER (Mason 1999), for example, evaluated 50 study support pilot schemes, Playing for Success (study support linked to professional football clubs), and a number of summer schools. The review reached the general conclusion that involvement in study support is associated with positive academic achievement – but the direction of effect is not clear: it may be that study support increases achievement, or equally, it may be that those who choose to attend out-of-hours activities are already more able or motivated than those who do not. There was evidence in Mason's study that pupils most likely to attend were those who perceived themselves as able, and who intended to remain in full-time education after the age of 16, and were from educationally advantaged homes.

Those involved in providing study support perceived benefits for pupils in terms of motivation, achievement, self-esteem, and improved personal and social skills. 'Hard' evidence of impact is lacking, however, except from the NFER evaluation of the Playing for Success initiative (Sharp *et al.* 2002), where improvements of, on average, 14 to 18 months in numeracy and 15 months in reading comprehension in primary-aged pupils (though not secondary) were reported.

Another research overview (Schwartz 1996) has identified features which need to be in place if study support is to be effective:

- programmes should have clear goals and strong links with the school curriculum;
- wherever possible, schools should use existing teaching staff to run the programmes, if children's school performance is to be improved;

- variety in activities (for example, building in sporting and cultural activities) can be important in developing new skills and raising self-esteem); and
- families should be involved in designing after-school schemes: children are more likely to attend if their families have been involved.

Breakfast clubs provide a morning meal for children who might otherwise start the day without one; some clubs also offer study support or play activities, while others focus on informal interaction to build relationships between adults and children and start the day in a positive climate. They have been evaluated by the New Policy Institute (2002). The evaluation found that children attending were reported by teachers to be more alert in the classroom and had improved social skills and concentration and improved school attendance. Positive changes in children's behaviour were not consistently found.

Interventions for children with social, emotional and behavioural difficulties

Social skills training

Structured group work to help children solve the problems that they experience in social settings is effective for older children, just as we have seen earlier in this chapter in the context of early intervention.

Major research reviews, such as those by Carr (2000), Kazdin (2000) and Buchanan (1999) have concluded that social skills group work is effective for children with the broad range of conduct disorders, for children with attention deficit hyperactivity disorder, and for adolescents at risk of exclusion from school.

As with younger children, combining social skills group work with some kind of work with parents/carers to help them learn new behaviour management skills is often more effective than work with the children and young people alone.

Social skills group work may focus on:

- friendship skills (how to make and keep friends, or deal with peer rejection and teasing);
- learning how to prevent or resolve conflict, and manage angry feelings; or
- learning how to manage relationships with adults – particularly teachers – in programmes with titles such as 'School Survival'.

Groups need to be small (usually about five to eight) and are run by a trained adult or pair of adults. Sessions often take place once a week for approximately eight to ten weeks, but there is evidence (Carr 2000) that longer programmes are more successful. The content usually includes some direct teaching and modelling, together with opportunities for discussion and practice within the sessions and outside.

Mentoring

Mentoring covers a range of interventions, from linking a child or young person with a volunteer adult (perhaps from a local business) who simply spends regular time with and shows interest in the child to sustained inputs from paid adults who have had intensive training in providing one-to-one pastoral support.

The common element in these schemes is that they offer children the unconditional friendship of a supportive adult, who takes a personal interest in their lives as a whole (not only the parts that happen in school), provides them with a role model and can help them reach self-determined goals.

The evidence on mentoring is mixed; outcomes appear to depend on the level of intervention and the extent of training the mentors receive. A scheme called Chance UK, which works with children of 5 to 11 with a variety of behaviour problems, and provides volunteer mentors with a three-day training programme, has not been found to produce greater improvements in children's behaviour than those found in a control group who did not have mentors – even though teachers and children themselves, and their families, rated the project highly (St James-Roberts and Singh 2002). A similar lack of impact has been found when children's academic achievements and other measures are used to evaluate the programme: a study at Durham University, for example, found that under-achieving 15-year-olds who were mentored actually did worse in their GCSEs than similar pupils who had no extra help.

In contrast, evaluations of a mentoring programme called Schools Outreach, which recruits full-time workers from the community served by a school and provides them with intensive diploma-level training in pastoral care before placing them in the school, are more positive in terms of impact on behavioural measures. Early indications are that the paid, school-based Learning Mentors funded under the DfES Excellence in Cities scheme are also having a significant impact on attainment, attendance and exclusion rates. An audit of mentoring schemes carried out by Manchester Metropolitan University concluded that the factors fundamental to success included real commitment by the school to the mentoring process, recognition by teachers of what mentors do, enough time and suitable venues for mentoring sessions and structured evaluation (Wilce 2002). Research in the USA suggests that mentoring programmes are unlikely to be effective if they rely only on building a supportive relationship: specific targets for behavioural change and a system of rewards and sanctions (contingencies) for meeting them may also be necessary (Fo and O'Donnell 1975).

Stress management and counselling

Another form of intervention aimed at preventing social, emotional and behavioural difficulty starts from the assumption that children, particularly in areas of high social deprivation, can experience intense stress in their lives and are likely to benefit from opportunities for stress reduction and relaxation. The best-known programme is called The Place to Be. Schools involved in this programme set up a special room, equipped with art and play materials, where volunteer adults with counselling skills work with children who are referred by teachers. Children – and adults – can also use the room at certain times on a self-referral, drop-in basis. The room aims to provide a setting which is calm and safe, where communication with trained listeners about emotions is encouraged.

Teachers value the programme highly; in an evaluation of work in 28 schools over a period of a year they reported that 87 per cent of the children involved showed positive change. 'Hard' evidence in the form of measures of attendance, attainment and exclusion has not so far been reported.

A similar scheme in Liverpool, called The Quiet Place, has been the subject of a rigorous evaluation which compared outcomes for children who had support with those of a control group which did not. The Quiet Place project designated a room in each of 17 primary schools, which offered a relaxing and aesthetically pleasing environment, rich in sensory stimulation such as twinkling lights, soft music and soothing waterfalls. The room provided the base for a six-week intervention with referred children, consisting of one session of psychotherapy, one session of 'therapeutic touch' and one session of relaxation training per week. The children involved in the programme made significantly greater gains than the control group in behaviour (concentration, self-esteem, impulse control, interpersonal skills, cooperativeness) as rated by independent observers and teachers (Renwick and Spalding 2002). The programme was slightly more effective with boys than with girls, and with older children (Years 4 to 6) than with younger children (nursery to Year 3).

Learning support units

Learning support units, or in-school behaviour support centres, are a growing phenomenon, particularly in the secondary sector. Such centres vary widely in the type of provision they make, from acting as a drop-in facility for students to use when under stress or at risk of getting into confrontation, to full-time teaching on an alternative curriculum. All have in common the presence of adults with skills in behaviour management (usually a mixture of teachers and teaching assistants or learning mentors); some are also able to offer counselling, group work or one-to-one cognitive-behavioural approaches to helping students find solutions to problems and to learn new skills in managing feelings and behaviour. Depending on staffing, some are able to provide outreach support in regular classes for students who are gradually reintegrated from the centre or who attend the centre part-time.

Differences in the way in which in-school behaviour centres operate make it difficult to evaluate their overall impact. DfES evaluations (Hallam and Castle 1999) of initial pilots found that schools with in-school centres did succeed in reducing the number of permanent exclusions by a factor of 4.3 per cent in the same year that there was a national rise of 2 per cent. There was considerable variation in permanent exclusion figures, however, and not all the schools involved were successful in bringing numbers down.

Where the centres were functioning well and operating according to particular parameters defined by the researchers, there was evidence of a reduction in fixed-term exclusions, ranging from 22 per cent to 30 per cent over a two-year period.

Factors associated with success included:

- operating a combination of withdrawal of pupils from their classes for limited periods, and in-class support at other times;
- operating in ways which involved teachers outside the centre, so that there was a sense of partnership and shared ownership;
- active involvement of senior staff who were involved from the start in defining and later supporting the role of the in-school centre as a complement to (not a substitute for) existing provision aimed at reducing exclusions;
- parental involvement;
- the presence of a physical centre which could provide pupils with a focus and a sanctuary where necessary;
- pupil involvement in setting targets for themselves, monitoring their own behaviour, making choices and accepting responsibility; and
- good communication systems within the school.

Factors likely to prevent the in-school centre being a success include:

- being used for 'fire-fighting' (on-the-spot referral of children who are misbehaving in a lesson) or as a dumping ground;
- being used for long-term respite care; or
- being seen as an isolated bolt-on provision, rather than as an integral part of a whole-school behaviour and inclusion policy.

Conclusion

In this chapter we have looked at a range of provision for high incidence needs (learning difficulties and SEBD), in terms of their evidence for effectiveness. Schools which adopt a strategic approach to SEN will want to draw on this evidence in making choices about what will go in their provision map, each year, to meet the range of needs they have identified. This is not to say that they will *only* draw on those successful programmes and schemes reviewed here: if everyone did this, there would be no innovation, no chance to try out and test new ideas arising from, or appropriate to, particular school situations. Nor are the named programmes and schemes suggested here necessarily more likely to succeed than are some of the tailor-made approaches devised by teachers with a high degree of training and expertise for the individual children they work with. It is perfectly possible for such a teacher, for example, to pull together a successful customised package for a child with literacy or behaviour difficulties that draws on use of ICT with appropriate software, plus elements of a number of different teaching or therapeutic approaches. Nevertheless, that teacher will need to compare the progress made by children on his or her tailor-made programmes with that which research has shown can be achieved through 'off-the-peg', named schemes. Similarly, those who are creating wholly novel approaches will need to evaluate them rigorously, in order to be sure that the outcomes are at least as good as those available from existing methodologies.

In all this evaluation we need to get better at refining our knowledge about 'what works', so that we can begin to move away from blanket, 'one-size-fits-all' applications, towards a more differentiated approach. We need to know more about what will work for older versus younger children, boys versus girls, pupils from different socio-economic or ethnic backgrounds and pupils with different degrees of initial difficulty.

Currently we do not have enough answers to questions like these. Our strategic provision choices still have to be informed by relatively crude indicators, but even these will be a significant advance on the situation in most schools, where choices are relatively rarely informed by any kind of evidence of impact.

8 Beating bureaucracy: minimising unnecessary IEPs and paperwork

Bureaucracy is the enemy of strategic management: dealing with day-to-day pressures of records to keep, forms to fill in and meetings to schedule is what prevents managers from sitting back and taking stock of longer-term issues.

For SEN, the pressures of the day-to-day are particularly acute. As long as the focus of SEN work is on the individual, the operational issues of managing IEPs, reviews, meetings with external agencies, and requests for funding will tend to dominate the agenda in many schools.

In order to make time for strategic issues, managers have first to find ways of freeing themselves and their colleagues from the weight of bureaucracy which the SEN Code of Practice can engender. This chapter looks at how this might be achieved.

Who needs IEPs?

IEPs and their associated reviews are the main source of SEN bureaucracy in schools. The well-intentioned aims that every child with significant SEN should have an individual plan describing their needs and how those needs will be met has become unsupportable in a climate where schools are identifying very large tranches of their population as experiencing special educational needs – 21 per cent in primary schools in January 2002 and 19 per cent in secondary (DfES 2002b). Report after report has highlighted the oppressive weight of administration and paperwork generated by attempts to plan at the individual level for such large numbers of children.

> The writing and reviewing of IEPs is giving the greatest cause for concern to SENCOs in both primary and secondary schools.
>
> (*The SEN Code of Practice: Three years on* [Ofsted 1999b: 7])

There are many incentives in the current system, however, for producing large numbers of IEPs. The more children the school has identified with SEN, the more favourably its position in the league tables may be judged if it appears to be underachieving in its SAT or GCSE outcomes. The more and smarter the individual education plans, the more additional LEA funding that is likely to be attracted to the school via audit or statementing mechanisms. IEPs also receive heavy emphasis in inspections, as the visible indicator of what teachers do to meet SEN, easy to get hold of (in both literal and metaphorical senses) by Ofsted inspectors whose expertise in SEN may be limited.

IEPs on a large scale, however, soon become meaningless documents. Even if each IEP has only the three or four targets prescribed in the Code, no primary teacher with 33 children to teach, still less the secondary teacher encountering hundreds of children in the course of a week, can possibly remember even one target for each of the large number of children who may have an IEP. If they can't remember what the targets are, how can they possibly use them in any meaningful way to guide their teaching or the child's learning?

There is, moreover, no real evidence that IEPs in quantity are effective in terms of outcomes. There is a circularity in the annual governors' report to parents claiming proudly that children are achieving the targets set on their IEPs, when the targets are required to be set from the start as specific, measurable, **achievable**, realistic and time-constrained. Nationally, there has been no survey of the progress made by children with SEN, with or without IEPs, which uses any hard data on outcomes.

Where it has proved possible to bring about significant reductions in the numbers of children failing to achieve basic levels of literacy and numeracy, this has not been through having more children recorded with SEN, or more and better IEPs. Instead these gains have been produced by introducing particular forms of provision, as outlined in Chapter 7, which actually deliver improved attainment or adjustment.

This situation has prompted many schools to take another look at IEPs, seeking to reduce their numbers while at the same time holding fast to the many useful purposes they are intended to serve. Their successes – some of which are illustrated later in this chapter – rest on developing the skills of classroom and subject teachers so as to move many of the strategies formerly recorded on individual IEPs into the realm of what is 'normally available' to all children in inclusive classrooms. Since IEPs are only necessary to record what is additional to or different from this normally available provision, their use can then be restricted to that smaller number of children with less frequently occurring, more complex types of need, and for those situations where a genuinely interactive process involving child, parent and school staff in face-to-face planning and review meetings is needed in order to kick-start a previously 'stuck' situation. With fewer IEPs, the school will be able to make them more meaningful – both in terms of this initial interactive problem-solving process and in their everyday impact in the classroom – than the paper exercise to which they have often been reduced in current practice.

Holding on to key principles

In order to escape the IEP paper chase, schools may decide to take a conscious, explicit and well-documented decision to dispense with wholesale IEPs altogether and replace them with a new system. Such a system involves:

- planned whole-school screening and assessment procedures;
- class and subject teachers incorporating into their medium- and short-term planning the work that groups of lower attaining pupils, or groups with shared social, emotional and behavioural difficulties, will undertake in order to address identified group learning and personal/social objectives;
- rigorous whole-school monitoring of targets set for raising achievement of lower attaining pupils, and for promoting the inclusion of all pupils; and
- alignment of resources based on data analysis and on teacher planning for particular groups.

In schools like these the full, teacher-dependent IEP process can then focus only on those children who need a fresh, concerted, home–school impetus to move them on, and those with the most complex needs.

To make this system work it is necessary for schools to demonstrate that they can still meet all the intended purposes of the Code and that the helpful features of having individual planning and reviews have not been lost. Gross (2000) has indicated how this might be done; Table 8.1 summarises the key issues.

Involving and accounting to parents

The model shown in Table 8.1 emphasises the key role which IEPs play in providing information and an accountability system for parents. Attempts to reduce the number of IEPs held overall in a school ignore this aspect at their peril.

Parents and carers will not be content with a system that fails to answer the key questions they have about their child:

- Has s/he got a problem?
- Will s/he qualify for extra help?
- What form will that help take?
- How will I know if it is working?
- How can we help at home?

Currently, the system of recording individual children's SEN and writing IEPs for them answers at least some of these questions. If parents and carers are to buy into the less individualistic and more strategic approach advocated in this book, they will need answers provided in different ways.

One essential is a really good information leaflet for parents/carers, setting out the provision the school makes for children with SEN, and how that provision is matched to level of need. Figure 8.1 provides an example of such a leaflet.

The SEN information leaflet for parents needs to give a clear description of the school's system for screening all children to identify potential SEN. This will help to answer the first question which parents ask: 'Has my child got a problem?'

Table 8.1   Meeting the purposes of the SEN Code of Practice

Purpose of Code	Meeting the purpose other than by IEPs
To make sure that children's SEN are identified	Screening procedures used in every year group, to identify children who may need help in class to overcome barriers to learning, or access to additional provision from the school's provision map
To make sure that children's individual needs are assessed	SENCO trains/coaches colleagues in use of assessment tools. SEN policy and staff handbook sets out what is expected of all staff
To help staff and children identify key learning targets	Process of individual target setting with *all* children. SENCO advises colleagues on how to choose appropriate learning objectives for children functioning below expected age-related levels
To make sure that effective strategies are put in place to support the child	SENCO or school-based behaviour specialist provide training and advice to colleagues on what works for children with learning or behaviour difficulties
To make sure that parents/carers know what the school is doing to help their child, and to what effect	School's provision map sets out provision available; parents receive a highlighted version showing the provision their child is accessing. Regular testing/ assessment of progress, reported to parents
To make sure that parents/carers know how they can help at home	SENCO and curriculum specialists run workshops and implement projects – for example, a paired reading project, or workshops on managing challenging behaviour. Class teachers or tutors use home–school diary or planner for two-way communication
To ensure that all relevant staff know what the child's needs are and how they can help him or her reach targets	Children take responsibility, with help, for recording general information (what I do well/what I find hard/ what helps me most) and key personal targets in planners/notebooks, and sharing these with those who teach them
To ensure continuity when children move from one class or school to another	Pupil-managed information as above. Clear policy on transfer of personal and curriculum records on all children
To direct the deployment of limited school resources to the individual children with the greatest need	The school plans its provision map strategically, on the basis of annual data analysis and forecasting of need in each year group/class
To demonstrate action at school level as a condition to seeking help at School Action Plus or through a Statement	The school provides a copy of its SEN policy, showing the systems that are in place for screening, assessment, setting individual targets and monitoring individuals' progress. The provision a child has received is highlighted on successive provision maps. Information is copied from regular teacher lesson planning and home/school diaries or planners to show outcomes of additional provision/action

HENGROVE SCHOOL

SPECIAL NEEDS DEPARTMENT

A leaflet for Parents and Carers

HELPING TO IMPROVE BEHAVIOUR

The Base is a social skills area which aims to help students whose behaviour is preventing their own learning and the learning of others in their teaching groups.

First Base is for the most needy students who are unwilling to attend school. They would normally only attend Base.

Second Base is for students who find school very difficult. They go to some lessons but attend Base for up to four periods each day. These students will have individual timetables prepared for them.

SUPPORT GROUPS (Third Base)

We also run behaviour support groups. Students are withdrawn from normal lesson once or twice a week to look at issues around improving behaviour in lessons.

Retracking

Some students who have been excluded follow a retracking programme to help them manage their behaviour. They attend for a lesson a day over a two week period.

Work with outside Agencies

The Special Needs Department works closely with the Bristol Special Needs Service and the Psychology Service, based in Orchard house. We also have contact with the Welfare Office, Social Services and the child and family support service and the Careers Service.

PARENTS ARE WELCOME

At Hengrove we try wherever possible to include parents in any discussion we have about what is best for their children. Please feel free to phone at any time to talk about what we are doing for your child or arrange a meeting with your child's Keyworker. You may like to come in just to have a look around.

If you have a complaint...

If you are concerned that the school is not meeting the needs of your child, the first person you should contact is either your child's tutor or special needs Keyworker. For serious matters you may wish to speak to Mr .... (Head of Special Needs) or the Governor with responsibility for Special Needs – Mrs ....

The Special Needs Policy

This leaflet provides a summary of the provision the school makes for students with special needs. Far more detail is given in the school Special Needs Policy. A copy of this can be obtained from school.

Hengrove School Special Needs Dept

Hengrove School
Petherton Gardens
Hengrove
Bristol

Phone: 01275 836077
Fax: 01275 892710
Email: school@mail.hengrove.bristol.sch.uk

Special Educational Needs
At Hengrove School

What is a Special Educational Need?

If a child finds it difficult to read, to spell and do maths, or perhaps gets into trouble in school, he or she may need extra help beyond what they would normally get in class. These children are said to have a "Special Educational Need."

Individual Education Plans

Children with the most serious special educational needs will have an Individual Education Plan (IEP). This has targets that each child will try to reach. It also shows how the school will try and help the child reach these targets.

Termly Reviews

Each term, parents are invited in to school to talk about the IEP and the targets. Together, we can decide how well the plan been working and whether anything can be done to improve it.

The Keyworker

Each child with Special Needs has a "Keyworker" from the Special Needs Staff. This teacher will meet with the child and his or her parents, draw up the IEP and check that your child is getting the help he or she needs.

The Special Needs Department

Staff

The Special Needs Department is one of the largest departments in the school. It has nine teaching staff, ten Learning Support Assistants and a full time clerical assistant.

Rooms

The Department has a suite of five rooms in the old sixth form block and an adjacent classroom. These comprise four small teaching rooms, The Base, a Key Stage 4 learning support room, office and admin area.

Resources

The Department is well resourced with a wide variety of material to work with students at all levels. We have two multi-media computers in each classroom.

HIRB

The school is fortunate in having a Hearing Impairment Resource Base housed in the school. The Base has a full time member of staff and Learning Support Assistant.

How does the SEN Department help your child...

Students' reading, spelling and maths are tested on entry and then again at the end of each year.

Who gets extra help?

1. Students who are working at Level 2 or below on the National Curriculum. These children will probably have a reading and/or spelling level of less than 8.5 years. They may also have difficulty with maths.
2. Students who have a disability.
3. Students with emotional or behavioural difficulties.

Some of these students are already identified as needing extra support through a Statement of Special Educational Need or through the School's Special Educational Need Assessment (SSENA)

What sort of help is available...

Nurture Group

The students with the greatest difficulties in Year 7 join a Nurture Group for the first year, where they are taught by one teacher for most subjects.

Support Groups

Sometimes students who find learning difficult are placed in smaller support groups. They will follow the same curriculum as other students but at a slower rate. With fewer students in the group they get more teacher attention.

Withdrawal Groups

Some students can manage in most lessons but may need some extra help with reading or spelling. They may be taken out of a lesson to work as a part of a small group, normally for one or two lessons a week.

In class support

The school employs ten learning support assistants who go into lessons to help support students who find the work difficult and may need extra help in understanding the work.

Help outside lessons

The school is trying to increase the opportunities for students to improve their learning at other times: before school, during the lunch hour or after school.

Support at KS4

This year we have introduced some alternative options for students in Year 10. They will be able to follow programmes of work more directly related to the world of work, and will be able to spend some time at college and on extended work experience.

Figure 8.1 A leaflet for parents and carers

Table 8.2 Criteria for allocating additional support at School Action (primary)

	Language and literacy	Mathematics	Personal and social development		
			Interacting & working with others	Independent & organisational skills	Attention
YR Term 1	Baseline assessment at or below Stage 3 for language reading or writing	Baseline assessment at or below Stage 3 for mathematics	Less than level P5	Less than level P5	Less than level P6
YR Term 3 Y1 Term 1	• Less than 10 high frequency words • Less than 10 sound-to-symbol knowledge • Reading: < 5y 3m on Carver WRaPS test (Y1) • Writing: at or below P level 6 • Speaking/expression: below P level 6 • Listening/comprehension: below P level 6	Number: below P level 6	Less than level P6 Behaviour that restricts access to the curriculum on a daily basis	Less than level P6	Less than level P7
Y1 Term 3 Y2 Term 1	• Reading: < 6y 0m on Carver WRaPS test • Writing: below level 1C • Speaking /listening: below level 1C	Number: below level 1C	Less than level P7 Reaching final sanctions in school behaviour plan Behaviour that restricts own/others access to the curriculum on a daily basis	Less than level P7	Less than level P8
Y2 Term 3 Y3 Term 1	• Reading: < 7y 0m on Carver WRaPS test • KS1 SATs – at or below level 1 for reading or writing • Speaking /listening: below 1B	KS1 SATs – at or below level 1	Less than level P8	Less than level P8	Less than level P9
Y3 Term 3 Y4 Y5 Y6	• At any time if reading/spelling age is 18 months or more below chronological age • At any time if working at more than one NC level below level expected for year group	• At any time if working at more than one NC level below level expected for year group	Reaching final sanctions in school behaviour plan Behaviour that restricts own/others access to the curriculum on a daily basis Requires adult support to organise self to complete familiar tasks Unable to work without peer/adult support for more than 15 minutes		

This criteria map is a guide, for the purpose of making clear to parents/carers, children and school staff the levels at which children might be considered for extra help. The actual decisions, however, will depend on assessment of the child's rate of progress as set out in the SEN *Code of Practice*.

Table 8.3 Criteria for allocating additional support (secondary)

	Differentiated Teaching/ Pastoral Care	School Action	School Action Plus
Learning difficulties	Difficulties across all subjects, with literacy 8.0 to 9.0 on entry	Literacy and Numeracy 7.5–8.5 on entry – up to 9.5 by Year 9	Literacy and Numeracy 6.5–7.0 or 7.5–8.5 plus additional problems e.g. coordination
Specific learning difficulties	Difficulties in very specific areas only, e.g. spelling. Literacy scores adrift by 2–3 years from ability; bigger gap may be seen in KS4	Difficulties in specific areas only, e.g. literacy. Attainment adrift from ability by 3–4 years	Attainment adrift by 5 years+ and other areas also of concern, e.g. dyspraxia, ADHD, behaviour
Attendance	Spasmodic absences mildly affecting learning; dealt with by tutor (80–90% attendance)	Absences which are more than spasmodic and may show a pattern; year head involved (70–80% attendance)	Very serious concern re. absences – lower than 50%; EWO involved
Medical	A mild difficulty which does not affect learning but which needs awareness, e.g. occasional fits/ deafness in one ear	A condition which can affect learning and needs monitoring as well as awareness, e.g. Crohn's Disease	A condition which is seriously affecting school work and requires regular medical interventions, e.g. serious head injury, regular fits
Emotional	An out-of-school issue which does not affect learning but which needs 'awareness'. Low-level but regular in-school worries which can be discussed with tutor	In- or out-of-school concerns which can affect attention to school work which need more intensive time with tutor or year head	As for School Action but requiring more regular and professional counselling. Seriously affecting school work
Behaviour and social adjustment	Irritating behaviour – subject lesson mentions 2/3 times a week. Can be dealt with by tutor	Subject lesson mentions 3–4 times a week, but with incident sheets 1–2 a week. Affects learning of class. Time with year head/SEBD support groups needed	Subject lesson mentions at least daily with incident sheets 2–3 times a week. Regularly brings others' learning to a halt and own learning seriously affected

To answer the question 'Will s/he qualify for extra help?' the SEN policy and leaflets can incorporate clear criteria for placing children on School Action. Examples, for primary and secondary schools, are given in Tables 8.2 and 8.3.

The school's provision map, duly highlighted to show the provision that will be put in place for a particular child, is likely to provide a better answer to the question 'What form will help take?' than an IEP, because it will encompass *all* the various forms of additional support which the child will access, rather than just those linked to three or four IEP targets.

The challenge for a more strategic, less individual, model, however, comes from the next question: 'How will we know if it is working?' The guarantee of an IEP review at least twice a year under the Code of Practice provides the accountability that may be absent where the targets for the child with SEN are no different from those set by every child for themselves in discussion with their teacher, and where the strategies to achieve them are recorded in whole-class curriculum planning and on the school's provision map. To meet this challenge, the school will need established systems for measuring the rate of progress of all children receiving additional support via the school's provision map, and reporting this routinely to parents/carers and to children themselves.

The tools for such measurement are the same as those used to evaluate the impact of the SEN provision at whole-school level: standardised tests, optional SATs, teacher assessment using 'P' scales or QCA behaviour ratings, measures of inclusion into the social community of the school.

Answering the last question, 'How can we help at home?', is more readily achieved than reporting on progress. Rather than work individually with each family on home support strategies, the school can offer workshops to groups of parents – on how to use a technique like paired reading to boost a child's literacy skills, for example, or on games to play at home to develop mathematical skills, or on appropriate ICT software for home use, or on how to help the child manage feelings and relationships. Such group events can allow the school to achieve economies of scale. They also capitalise on the powerful self-help effects engendered by any group process, as opposed to a process which only involves individuals.

CASE STUDY

Beating bureaucracy in a secondary school

One large secondary school decided to use the revision of the SEN Code of Practice in 2001 as an opportunity to reconsider ways of working. Before 2001, the school had around 100 IEPs, half of what some other local schools had, but still an unmanageable number in terms of writing, monitoring and reviewing – never mind implementation. As the SENCO said, 'The problem with IEPs, whether stored in teachers' individual planners, the SEN filing cabinet, a reference book in the staff room, in departmental offices, on the school intranet or even pasted into individual student diaries, is that they are rarely referred to except at the time of writing or reviewing. No matter what we did, we could not create proactive, working IEPs, so we were ready for a radical change. We found the original Code of Practice had created paper systems which, in the end, overwhelmed us, taking the focus off what we were providing and putting it on how we were accounting for what we were providing.'

Important considerations for the school in any new system were that students with SEN needed to be appropriately identified and their SEN recognised; teachers needed information on students and how to meet their particular needs; parents needed to be assured that the school would meet the needs of their child, and kept informed and involved; students needed ownership of their learning.

In the first instance, the school decided that IEPs would be written only for the 20 students with Statements, where clearly provision 'additional to or different from that normally available to all pupils' was being made. This felt to everyone like a manageable number of IEPs.

Secondly, that key phrase in the revised Code, 'additional to or different from. . .', allowed the school to consider what it already had in place as part of normal differentiated provision to meet the needs of a diverse student population. This includes a management system which involves each department having a named teacher with SEN responsibilities in the subject. The SENCO chairs a termly meeting of this SEN Liaison Group, and works regularly with each department through the named person. All departments have SEN as an agenda item at every department meeting. Each SEN representative has created a system within his/her department for managing and sharing information on students with SEN, and for disseminating information on teaching and learning in the subject relevant to different special needs

Differentiation for all students is a strength in the school. Every teacher accepts responsibility for every student in the class. Each subject works to the National Curriculum inclusion statement, which requires all teachers to set appropriate learning objectives for every student, to use different teaching styles in response to students' needs, and to ensure there are no barriers preventing students from accessing these appropriate learning objectives and teaching styles. Each department acknowledges this with an 'SEN policy' or statement in the department handbook, spelling out their responsibilities to include students with SEN as well as other vulnerable students.

Target-setting for students with SEN occurs in the normal context of target-setting for all:

- each teacher sets objectives for each lesson and shares them with students by writing them on the board at the beginning of each lesson;
- subject teachers will negotiate individually set targets with all students, specific to the subject and based on the work they produce and the difficulties they are having;
- form tutors have a period per fortnight for personal tutoring with members of their tutor group, to monitor progress towards the targets which students set in consultation with the form tutor and their parents; and
- in-class support allows LSAs to monitor students with SEN (and others), and to help them achieve their targets and recognise when a target is achieved or needs to be changed. LSAs also have target sheets which, if appropriate, can be stuck in students' planners to remind them of the targets on which they are currently working within that week/month/module.

Systems are in place to ensure that any difficulties which students may have are identified early. Literacy screening and numeracy assessment information is available on all students.

The school's provision map sets out its substantial provision for SEN. The weakest English sets in all Key Stage 3 years are targeted with individualised Phono-graphix™ intervention for those who need help with literacy. All teachers are familiar with Phono-graphix™ spelling strategies and use these to teach reading and spelling of key subject vocabulary to all students.

Work on study and organisational skills is specifically targeted at Key Stage 4 and sixth-form students with SEN, and delivered by a specialist teacher. A supported homework club is run at lunchtimes by LSAs for Key Stage 3 or Key Stage 4 students. ICT software to promote numeracy and literacy skills can be accessed at this time.

Learning support technology – access to laptop word-processors or tape-recorders, use of PCs or spellcheckers – is available to any student for use in lessons, although students with SEN may be particularly encouraged to take up this offer.

Behaviour issues are managed by form tutors and heads of year in conjunction with heads of key stage and the SENCO, working within a strong whole-school behaviour policy and within the system of target-setting with students by teachers, form tutors and LSAs, which is as likely to focus on social/behaviour targets as on those for learning.

In order to support access to the curriculum, Learning Support assistance is targeted to all weak sets in English, Maths and Science, to blocks of mixed-ability grouped Humanities, French and Technology lessons and to Music, Art or Drama lessons if a student would not be able to participate without it.

Most LSAs have one period per week as a non-contact link period to work on developing or modifying differentiated materials for a named subject area or sometimes a specific student. Many departments have run training sessions for LSAs to provide them with information on schemes of work, key concepts and how the department wants LSAs to support students in the subject.

A wide range of alternative curriculum options is available in Key Stage 4, including work experience for half a day per week and a whole day per week FE College option. KS4 students may select a Study Option instead of a modern foreign language. This option provides supported study, extra time for coursework and classwork, opportunities to improve literacy, numeracy or ICT skills, time for individual mentoring and a number of lessons designed to enhance self-esteem and confidence.

Students do not need to have IEPs in order to access this wide range of provision. The school is clear, however, that teachers still need to know which students have special needs and how the special need will affect teaching and learning. There is therefore an SEN Watch Out list which includes every student from those once classified as Stage 1 Concern to those with a Statement. This alerts all teachers to the fact that these are the students for whom they will need to take special care when considering learning objectives, teaching styles and access.

In addition, there are about 50 students from the Watch Out list for whom teachers need further information. This is provided on an individual A4 sheet called a Student Information Sheet (SIS). Figure 8.2 shows an example. The SIS always has four to five bullet points detailing the specific SEN concerns for the student and a similar number of bullet points providing information on the action teachers could consider taking to promote learning. The bottom half of the sheet is left for teachers to keep working notes under two headings: problems relevant to this subject and action taken to ensure success in the subject. This forms the review feedback provided to the learning support department in February and June and updated information for the next SIS, if one is needed. SISs are always discussed with students and parents at parents' evenings.

Parents are happy with the new system. Only one parent wanted to retain an IEP, as visible confirmation of the provision being made. She has since agreed that

Subject _____

Teacher _____

Name ___**TT**_____ TutGp __**8F**_____ Date _**Sept 02**_____

Areas of concern:

➤ Good average ability, but specific dyslexic difficulties affecting his literacy, especially spelling

➤ His good general knowledge and conceptual ability are masked by slow language processing and difficulties with organising ideas

➤ Keen and conscientious worker, but reading and particularly written work takes tremendous effort and time

➤ Written work often does not reflect his ability or his understanding, can be untidy and incomplete

Action: *(To include helpful strategies, information or SMART targets to promote learning)*

➤ Provide extra time and support for processing oral responses, reading and written work

➤ Accept alternative presentation (drawings, bullet points, word processed, etc.); provide key word list

➤ He is proficient at word processing and uses a hand-held PC in lessons – support him to make judgements on when it is appropriate to use ICT or to handwrite; help him organise/present word processed work appropriately (possibly by providing A4 file rather than by pasting in exercise books)

➤ He finds using a coloured overlay helpful when reading

➤ Marking all over his work in red pen is intimidating and discouraging to him; mark so that he is encouraged to focus on one subject-specific target at a time to improve presentation, spelling, etc.

➤ He works regularly with CM on literacy skills; now knows good strategies for helping himself to read and write difficult words, e.g. chunking syllables and 'scratch sheet spelling'

Review date: _____**3 Feb 03**_____
Return a photocopy of this form with bottom box completed to _____CM_____ by this date.

Teacher's working notes

➤ Problems relevant to this subject:

➤ Action taken to ensure success in subject:

Figure 8.2 Student information sheet

the IEP is no longer necessary to ensure that all teachers are dealing appropriately with her child.

The school are clear about the benefits of reducing bureaucracy: there is now much more time for the learning support department to work directly with students and staff. As the SENCO says, 'I feel that the important thing is to ensure every department and every teacher recognises and accepts their responsibilities for students with SEN, and the role of my department is to actively support teachers and students to ensure this is happening. The way we now work has made this possible.'

9 Developing staff: the SENCO and management team

Managing and developing staff successfully is fundamental to the process of school improvement. For SEN it will involve performance management and professional development for class and subject teachers, teaching and learning support assistants, lunchtime supervisors, SENCOs and senior managers, including the head teacher.

Figure 9.1 The school improvement cycle

A number of excellent texts have been written recently (e.g., Jones *et al*. 2002) to help SENCOs, in particular, with their growing role in managing and developing staff. It is not the intention to repeat this advice here. Instead, we will focus on managing the group of staff about whom little has been written: SENCOs themselves, and the other key managers who work with the SENCO to develop policy, practice and provision for children with SEN in the school.

In this final chapter we will look at tools which can form part of their professional development process.

SENCO Self-Audit

The first tool in this chapter (Figure 9.2) is a tool which SENCOs can use to identify their own professional development needs. It takes the form of a simple checklist, with three choices ('I am good at this'/'I can do this OK'/'I need to develop in this area') plotted against each of the SENCO competencies identified by the TTA Specialist SENCO Standards.

Managing the SENCO

The second tool in this chapter (Figure 9.3) is a tool for head teachers. Devised by an experienced SEN Adviser (Berger 2000) it outlines an annual performance management cycle for the head teacher and other senior

113

LIVERPOOL JOHN MOORES UNIVERSITY
LEARNING SERVICES

Table 9.1 SENCO self-audit against the national TTA standards

Competencies Checklist			
Competency	I am good this	I can do this OK	I need to develop in this area
• Know the characteristics of effective teaching			
• Use ICT			
• Keep up to date with subject			
• Communicate effectively			
• Coordinate and provide training for staff			
• Manage IEPs well			
• Analyse and interpret data			
• Help staff to set realistic expectations			
• Disseminate good practice			
• Monitor and evaluate the provision made for pupils with SEN, including the effectiveness of teaching and learning			
• Support literacy, numeracy, ICT and other developments			
• Support pupils in becoming independent and using study skills			
• Manage transition effectively			
• Collect and interpret assessment data			
• Devise, implement and evaluate SEN systems			
• Provide regular information for HT and governors on the effectiveness of provision for pupils with SEN			
• Help staff understand the needs of pupils with SEN and achieve constructive working relationships with them			
• Monitor pupils' progress			
• Set up meetings to review pupils' progress against the targets set			
• Develop partnership with parents			
• Develop effective liaison with other agencies			
• Chair meetings effectively			
• Manage time effectively			
• Be responsible for own development			
• Deploy resources effectively			
• Maintain resources and explore opportunities for new resources			
• Ensure SDP includes developments resulting from SEN policy objectives			

Table 9.1 *Continued*

Competency	I am good this	I can do this OK	I need to develop in this area
• Contribute to the positive ethos of the school			
• Know how to recognise and deal with stereotyping in relation to disability or race			
• Advise head teacher and governing body on the level of resources needed to maximise the achievement and progress of pupils with SEN, and on priorities			
• Allocate resources efficiently to achieve objectives			
• Use specialist knowledge to assess the needs of children with difficulties in cognition and learning, and advise on/ use appropriate teaching approaches			
• Use specialist knowledge to assess the needs of children with physical or sensory impairment, or medical needs, and advise on/ use appropriate teaching approaches			
• Use specialist knowledge to assess the needs of children with difficulties in communication and interaction, and advise on/ use appropriate teaching approaches			
• Use specialist knowledge to assess the needs of children with social, emotional or behavioural, difficulties and advise on/ use appropriate teaching approaches			

managers to follow. The cycle begins with the head teacher and SENCO analysing, together, the outcomes for pupils with SEN in statutory and optional tests and teacher assessment, along with other outcomes on measurable targets which the school has set for itself in terms of achievement, behaviour and inclusion. At the same time the SENCO audits his or her knowledge and skills against the TTA standards. All this information is used by the head teacher and SENCO to develop a brief action plan and associated training plan. Subsequently, performance management targets are agreed and followed up at the end of the cycle, with a management observation of key areas of the SENCO's work.

Table 9.2 Managing the SENCO

The annual management cycle

SENCO responsibilities:
- day-to-day management of SEN provision
- professional guidance to staff on SEN

Outcomes:
- high-quality inclusive teaching
- efficient use of resources
- improved standards

Time	Activity
June – September	SENCO results meeting Data analysis SENCO self audit against TTA standards
July – September	Action planning to address identified areas for development
October	Non-contact time allocation Training programme agreed
November – December	Targets agreed
October – May	SENCO implements action plan, undertakes relevant training
April – May	Management observation
June	Performance management meetings

Note: Some schools plan on a different cycle and these months are only suggestions. The cycle should fit into the cycle for managing subject leaders.

Table 9.3   SENCO Development Plan

Date

Identified area for development		
Actions	**Costs**	**Outcomes**
Evaluation arrangements		

Non-contact time allocation

Date	Activity	Outcome

Table 9.4 Setting SEN targets

Examples	Targets
Increase percentage of pupils attaining level 1 / 3 / 4s (KS1, 2, 3) 'P' level gains Improvements in reading/writing or mathematics levels (targets to include at least two months' gain for every chronological month/improved attainment for children receiving additional support)	
Improvements in behaviour, e.g., • levels of fixed-term exclusion • numbers on part-time attendance • numbers of lunchtime exclusions • movement on the QCA behaviour scales • numbers of pupils who have to have additional behaviour provision	
Inclusion, e.g., • decrease in pupils leaving school to attend a special school or unit • measures of social interaction in classes where there are children with complex needs • measures of curriculum access	

Table 9.5 Conducting a management observation

Prompt	Evidence
Record of pupils with SEN • efficiently kept monitored	
IEPs • clear targets • focus on outcomes • appropriate action	
Organisation • management of reviews • involvement of parents and pupils • maintaining and analysing data • identifying and contributing to colleagues' professional development • observing teaching and feeding back to colleagues • reviewing teachers' planning	
Quality of any specialist teaching delivered by SENCO • delivery of focused, structured programmes • good planning of learning objectives • interactive teaching using multisensory resources • fast pace of sessions	
Scrutiny of pupils' work, where SENCO delivers specialist teaching • pace • presentation • progress	

Conclusion

And now we come to the end of one cycle of school improvement in relation to SEN, and the beginning of another. If you have worked through the chapters in this book, you will have in place a robust sense of where your school is in those aspects of inclusion which relate to SEN, in relation to national and local comparators, and national and local policy directions. You will have identified areas where you need to take action so as to adjust to changing contexts, and to improve

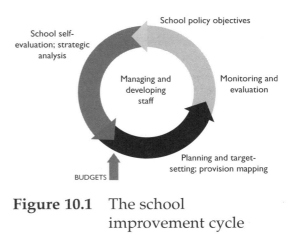

Figure 10.1 The school improvement cycle

outcomes. You will have planned your SEN provision through a logical and systematic process that draws on your analysis of present and future need in the school, and is informed by up-to-date information on the types of provision which are likely to be effective. There will be a system in place to monitor and evaluate both provision and school improvement plans; performance management will tie in, at all points, with your agreed strategic definition of where you want to take the school in its work to include and raise standards for learners with SEN.

Perhaps even more importantly, you should have in place a system that raises standards and promotes inclusion without depending on a heavyweight bureaucracy of individual plans and paperwork. You will be focusing on outcomes rather than procedures; on action rather than process; on action that is early and tackles difficulties before they become entrenched rather than on action that comes late and is, consequently, less effective.

As a result of your work, you will be achieving what the school improvement process is fundamentally all about – better outcomes for children, and, in this case, for that group of children who count among our most vulnerable.

Further information

This section gives details of where to find out more about SEN programmes and interventions referred to in the text.

AcceleRead, AcceleWrite
Talking Systems
22 Heavitree Road
Exeter
Devon EX1 2LQ
talksystem@aol.com

Better Reading Partnerships
Carol Taylor – Director
Read on – Write Away!
County Hall
Matlock
Derbyshire DE4 3AG
carol@rowa.co.uk
www.rowa.co.uk

Catch Up Project
Julie Lawes
Project Director
Thetford EAZ
Baxter Healthcare
Caxton Way
Thetford
Norfolk IP24 3SE
Catchup.eaz@virgin.net
www.thecatchupproject.org

Dinosaur School and Webster Stratton parenting programmes
Contact your local child and family guidance/child and adolescent psychiatric service

Family Links Nurturing Programme
Family Links
New Marston Centre
Jack Straws Lane
Oxford OX3 0DL
familylinksuk@aol.com

Family Literacy and Numeracy
Basic Skills Agency
Commonwealth House
1–19 New Oxford Street
London WC1A 1NU
www.basic-skills.co.uk

Mathematics Recovery
James Martland
University of Liverpool
Department of Education
Liverpool L69 3BX
www.liv.ac.uk/education/mathrec

Multi-sensory Teaching System for Reading (MTSR)
Mike Johnson
Manchester Metropolitan University
Institute of Education
799 Wilmslow Road
Manchester M20 2RR
www.mmu.ac.uk/ioe/projects/mtsr/mtsrl.html

National Pyramid Trust
84 Uxbridge Road
London W13 8RA
enquiries@nptrust.org.uk

Nurture Groups
Marion Bennathan
24 Murray Mews
London NW1 9RJ
Awcebd2@mistral.co.uk

**Paired Reading, Cued Spelling,
Paired Writing and Maths**
Professor Keith Topping
Centre for Paired Learning
Department of Psychology
University of Dundee
Dundee DD1 4HN
*http//www.Dundee.ac.uk/psychology/
TRW/resources*

Phono-graphix
http://www.readamerica.net

Reading Recovery
Reading Recovery National Network
Institute of Education
20 Bedford Way
London WC1H 0AL
Readrec@ioe.ac.uk

The Place to Be
Edinburgh House
154–182 Kennington Lane
London SE11 4EZ
P2B@compuserve.com

The Quiet Place
Department of Education
19 Abercromby Square
Liverpool
L69 7ZG

Reciprocal Teaching
Christa Rippon
Principal Educational Psychologist
London Borough of Haringey
Haringey Professional Development
Centre
Downhills Park Road
London N17 6AR

Schools Outreach
10 High Street
Bromsgrove
Worcestershire B61 8HQ
Schools.outreach@mcmail.com

Talking Partners
Education Bradford
Literacy and Language Team
TF Davies Centre
Rosemount, Clifton Villas
Manningham Lane
Bradford BD8 7BY
Jan.hilditch@bradford.gov.uk

Teaching Talking
Published by NFER-Nelson and
available from their education
catalogue.

THRASS
THRASS UK Ltd
Units 1–3 Tarvin Sands
Barrow Lane
Tarvin
Chester CH3 8JF
http://www.thrass.co.uk

**The Whole School Quality Circle
Time Model**
Jenny Mosley
Whole School Quality Circle Time
28A Gloucester Road
Trowbridge
Wiltshire
BA14 0AA
circletime@jennymosley.demon.co.uk

Valued Youth Project
www.youthesteem-uk.org

You Can Do It
Prospects Education Services
Head Office
7th floor
Grosvenor House
125 High Street
Croydon CR0 9XP
Sue.overy@prospects.co.uk

References

Aram, D. and Nation, J. (1980) 'Preschool language disorders and subsequent language and academic difficulties'. *Journal of Communication Disorders,* **13.**

Archer, T., Fletcher-Campbell, F. and Kendall, L. (2002) *Annual Survey of Trends in Education: Digest no. 12.* Slough: NFER.

Barber, M. (1996) *The Learning Game: Arguments for an education revolution.* London: Victor Gollancz.

Barlow, J. (1999) *Systematic Review of the Effectiveness of Parent-training Programmes in Improving Behaviour Problems in Children aged 3–10 Years.* Oxford: Health Services Research Unit, Department of Public Health.

Barlow, J. and Stewart-Brown, S. (1999) *Pilot Study of a Home–school Linked Parent Training Programme.* Oxford: Health Services Research Unit, Department of Public Health.

Barnard, M. (2000) *You Can Do It!* California: You Can Do It.

Bennathan, M. and Boxall, M. (2000) *Effective Interventions in Primary Schools: Nurture groups.* London: David Fulton.

Bennett, N. (1998) 'Annotation: class size and the quality of educational outcomes'. *Journal of Child Psychology and Psychiatry,* **39,** 6.

Berger, A. (2000) Personal communication.

Black, P., Harrisson, C., Lee, C., Marshall, B. and Wiliam, D. (2002)*Working Inside the Black Box.* London: Kings College.

Blatchford, P., Burke, J., Farquahar, C. *et al.* (1989) 'Teacher expectations in the infant school', *British Journal of Educational Psychology,* **59** (1).

Blatchford, P., Martin, C., Moriarty, V., Bassett, P. and Goldstein, H. (2002) *Pupil Adult Ratio Differences and Educational Progress over Reception and Key Stage 1.* London: DfES.

Blatchford, P. and Mortimore, P. (1994) 'Issue of class size for young children in schools: what can we learn from research?' *Oxford Review of Education,* **20.**

Brooks, G. (2002) *What Works for Children with Literacy Difficulties.* London: DfES.

Brooks-Gunn, J. (2001) *What Do We Know about Children's Development from Theory, Intervention and Policy?* Paper for the Jacobs Foundation, Zurich.

Buchanan, A. (1999) *What Works for Troubled Children.* London: Barnardo's.

Campbell, F. and Ramey, C. (1994) 'Effects of early intervention on intellectual and academic achievement: a follow-up study from low-income families'. *Child Development,* **65.**

Carr, A. (ed.) (2000) *What Works for Children and Adolescents: A critical review of psychological interventions with children, adolescents and their families.* London: Routledge.

Centre for Studies on Inclusive Education (CSIE) (2002) *Index for Inclusion: developing learning and participation in schools.* Bristol: CSIE.

Chapman, J., Tunmer, W. and Prochnow, J. (1998) *Reading Recovery in Relation to Language Factors, Reading Self-perceptions, Classroom Behaviour Difficulties and Literacy Achievement: A longitudinal study.* Paper presented to AERA, San Diego, CA, April.

Charlton, T. (1998) 'Enhancing school effectiveness through using peer support'. *Support for Learning,* **13**, 2.

Cheminais, R. (2001) *Developing Inclusive School Practice: A practical guide.* London: David Fulton.

Dann, V. (2002) 'Education action zone boosts speech and language skills'. *Afasic Abstract,* Spring.

Davies, G. (2000) 'The Coca-Cola (cross-age tutoring) valued youth programme as an inclusive strategy. Paper presented to the International Special Education Congress.

Derington, C., Evans, C. and Lee, B. (1996) *The Code in Practice: The impact on schools and LEAs.* Slough: NFER.

DfEE (1998) *Meeting Special Educational Needs: A programme of action.* London: DfEE.

DfES (2001a) *Special Educational Needs Code of Practice.* London: DfES.

DfES (2001b) *Inclusive Schooling: Children with special educational needs.* London: DfES.

DfES (2002a) *Accessible Schools: Planning to increase access to schools for disabled pupils.* London: DfES.

DfES (2002b) *Special Educational Needs in Schools in England: January 2002.* London: DfES.

DfES (2002c) *Including All Children in the Literacy Hour and Daily Mathematics Lesson: A management guide.* London: DfES .

DfES/Coram Family (2002) *Intervening Early.* London: DfES.

DfES/QCA (2001) *Supporting the Target Setting Process* (revised March 2001). London: DfES publications.

Dowker, A. (2001) 'Interventions in numeracy: the development of a numeracy recovery project for young children with arithmetical difficulties'. *Support for Learning,* **16**.

Farrell, P., Balshaw, M. and Polat, F. (1999) *The Management, Role and Training of Learning Support Assistants.* London: DfEE.

Fo, W. and O'Donnell, C. (1975) 'The buddy system: relationship and contingency conditioning as a community intervention programme for youth'. *Journal of Consulting and Clinical Psychology,* **42**.

Gallagher, A., Frith, U. and Snowling, M. (2000) 'Precursors of literacy delay among children at genetic risk of dyslexia'. *Journal of Child Psychology and Psychiatry,* **41**.

Gardner, H. (1993) *Multiple Intelligences: The theory in practice.* New York: Basic Books.

Gross, J. (2000) 'Paper promises'. *Support for Learning*, **15** (3).

Gross, J. (2002) *Special Educational Needs in the Primary School: A practical guide.* Buckingham: Open University Press.

Hallam, S. (1996) *Grouping Pupils by Ability: Selection, streaming, banding and setting.* London: Institute of Education.

Hallam, S. and Castle, F. (1999) *Evaluation of the Behaviour and Discipline Pilot Projects (1996–99) Supported under the Standards Fund Programme.* London: DfEE.

Hanushek, E. (1997) 'The evidence on class size'. *Wallen Wallis Institute of Political Economy, University of Rochester, Working Paper No. 10.* Rochester, NY: University of Rochester.

Harlen, W. and Deakin Crick, R. (2002) 'A systematic review of the impact of summative assessment and tests on pupils' motivation for learning (EPPI-Centre Review), in *Research Evidence in Education Library*, Issue 1. London: EPPI-Centre, Social Science Research Unit, Institute of Education.

Harlen, W. and Malcolm H. (1999) *Setting and Streaming: A research review.* Glasgow: Scottish Council for Research in Education.

Hilditch, J. (2002) Personal communication.

Horner, E. (1990) 'Working with peers'. *Special Children*, November.

Howson, J. (2002) 'Everyone hires more supporters'. *Times Educational Supplement*, 3 May.

Hurry, J. and Sylva, K. (1998) *The Long Term Effects of Two Interventions for Children with Reading Difficulties.* London: QCA.

Iszatt, J. and Wasilewska, T. (1997) 'Nurture groups: an early intervention model'. *Educational and Child Psychology*, **14**, 3.

Jones, F., Jones, K., and Szwed, C. (2002) *The SENCO as Teacher and Manager.* London: David Fulton Publishers.

Kazdin, A. (2000) 'Treatments for aggressive and antisocial children', in Lewis, D. and Yeager, C. (eds) *Child and Adolescent Clinics of North America*, **9**.

Krueger, A. (1999) 'Experimental estimates of education production functions' *Quarterly Journal of Economics*, **114**, 2.

Leeves, I. (1990) 'Now hear this'. *Special Children*, April.

Levin, H. and Glass, G. (1986) 'The political arithmetic of cost-benefit analysis'. *Phi Delta Kappa*, **68**, 1.

Locke, A., Ginsborg, J. and Peers, I. (2002) 'Development and disadvantage: implications for early years and beyond'. *International Journal of Language and Communication Disorders*, **37**, 1.

Locke, A. and Beech, M. (1991) *Teaching Talking.* Windsor : NFER-Nelson.

Lorenz, S. (1999) *Effective In-class Support.* London: David Fulton.

McLelland, N. (2002) *National Literacy Trust Early Language Campaign.* London: National Literacy Trust.

Maher, C. (1984) 'Handicapped adolescents as cross-age tutors'. *Exceptional Children*, **51**.

Makins, V. (1997) *The Invisible Children*. London: David Fulton/National Pyramid Trust.

Mason, K. (1999) 'What is study support? What does it have to offer?' *NFER News*, Autumn.

MENCAP (1999) *On a Wing and a Prayer*. London: MENCAP.

Moore, M. and Wade, B. (1998). 'Reading Recovery: its effectiveness in the long term'. *Support for Learning*, **13**, 3.

Morris E. (2002) 'Emotional literacy – releasing potential'. *Special Children*, October.

Mosley, J. (1993) *Turn Your School Around*. Wisbech, LDA.

New Policy Institute (2002) *A National Evaluation of Breakfast Clubs*. London: New Policy Institute. (On-line report at www.breakfastclubs.net)

Ofsted (1999a) *Setting in Primary Schools*. London: Ofsted.

Ofsted (1999b) *The SEN Code of Practice: Three years on*. London, Ofsted.

Ofsted (2001) *Evaluating Educational Inclusion*. London: Ofsted.

Ofsted (2002) *Teaching Assistants in Primary Schools: An Evaluation of the Quality and Impact of Their Work*. London: Ofsted.

Ofsted and Audit Commission (2002) *LEA Strategy for the Inclusion of Pupils with Special Educational Needs*. London: Ofsted.

Osborne and Gaebler (1992), quoted in *Aiming to Improve: The principles of performance measurement* (2002). London: Audit Commission.

Pinnell, G., Lyons, C., DeFord, D., Bryk, A. and Seltzer, M. (1994) 'Comparing instructional models for the literacy education of high-risk first graders'. *Reading Research Quarterly*, **29**, 1.

QCA (2001) *Supporting School Improvement: Guidance on setting improvement targets for pupils' emotional and behavioural development*. London: QCA.

Reading Recovery National Network (2001) *Annual Monitoring September 2000 to July 2001*. London: Institute of Education.

Renwick, F. and Spalding, B. (2002) 'The Quiet Place project: an evaluation of early therapeutic intervention in mainstream schools'. *British Journal of Special Education*, **29**, 3.

St James-Roberts, I. and Singh, C. (2002) *Mentors for Primary School Children with Behaviour Problems: An evaluation of the CHANCE project*. London: Home Office.

Schwartz, W. (1996) *After School Programmes for Urban Youth*. ERIC/CUE Digest no. 114. New York: Education Resources Information Centre.

Sharp, C., Blackmore, J., Kendall, L. *et al.* (2002) *Playing for Success: An evaluation of the third year*. London: DfES.

Sheridan, M. and Peckham, C. (1975) 'Follow up at 11 years of children who had marked speech defects at 7 years'. *Child Care and Health Development*, **113**.

Skinner, C. (1996) *Evaluation of the Effectiveness of National Pyramid Trust Clubs held in 1995–6*. Guildford: University of Surrey.

Sutherland, J. and Topping, K. (1999) 'Collaborative creative writing in eight year olds: comparing cross-ability fixed role and same-ability reciprocal role pairing'. *Journal of Research in Reading*, **22**, 2.

Sukhnandan, L. and Lee, B. (1998) *Streaming, Setting and Grouping by Ability.* Slough: NFER.

Tennant, G. (2001) 'The rhetoric and reality of learning support in the classroom: towards a synthesis'. *Support for Learning,* **16**, 4.

Thomas, G. and Tarr, J. (1996) *The Monitoring and Evaluation of Schools' SEN Policies: A report of a research project conducted for the DfEE.* London: DfEE.

Topping, K. and Ehly, S. (1998) *Peer Assisted Learning.* London: Lawrence Erlbaum.

Webster-Stratton, C. and Hammond, M. (1997) 'Treating children with early-onset conduct problems: a comparison of child and parent training interventions'. *Journal of Consulting and Clinical Psychology,* **65**, 1.

Webster-Stratton, C., Reid, J. and Hammond, M. (2001) 'Social skills and problem-solving training for children with early-onset conduct problems: Who benefits?' *Journal of Child Psychology and Psychiatry,* **42**, 7.

Whitburn, J. (2001) 'Effective classroom organisation in primary schools: mathematics'. *Oxford Review of Education,* **27**, 3.

Wilce, H. (2001) 'Amazing mainstream'. *Times Educational Supplement,* 6 July.

Wilce, H. (2002), *The Independent,* 6 June 2002.

Wright, R., Martland, J. and Stafford, A. (2000) *Early Numeracy: Assessment for teaching and intervention.* London: Paul Chapman.

Appendix: School improvement and SEN training materials

The Powerpoint slides in this appendix can be downloaded from the David Fulton Publishers website (www.fultonpublishers.co.uk) using the password 'sensim'.

School improvement and special educational needs: practical strategies to raise standards

Aims

- To consider how to apply to SEN the tools for school improvement which have proved successful for the broad majority of pupils

Aims

- To look at good practice in target setting
- To consider how to conduct self evaluation
- To identify areas for school development planning

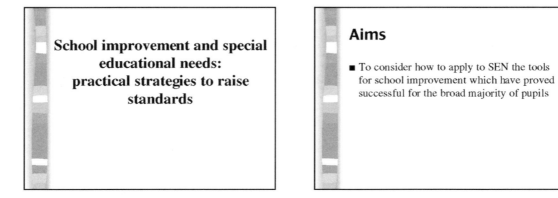

The school improvement cycle

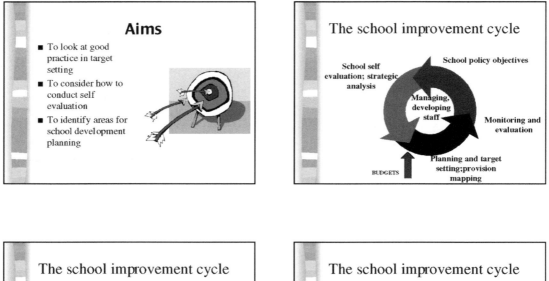

School self evaluation; strategic analysis

School policy objectives

Managing, developing staff

Monitoring and evaluation

Planning and target setting; provision mapping

BUDGETS

The school improvement cycle

What do we want to achieve, in the long term, for pupils with SEN in our school?

School policy objectives

The school improvement cycle

How well are we doing?
How do we compare with similar schools?
How well should we be doing?
What changes are going on in the environment and how might they affect us?
What is the current and future profile of SEN need within the school?

School self evaluation; strategic analysis

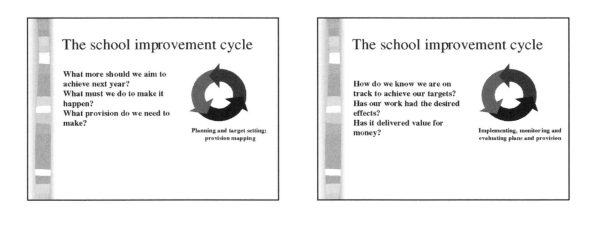

The school improvement cycle

What more should we aim to achieve next year?
What must we do to make it happen?
What provision do we need to make?

Planning and target setting; provision mapping

The school improvement cycle

How do we know we are on track to achieve our targets?
Has our work had the desired effects?
Has it delivered value for money?

Implementing, monitoring and evaluating plans and provision

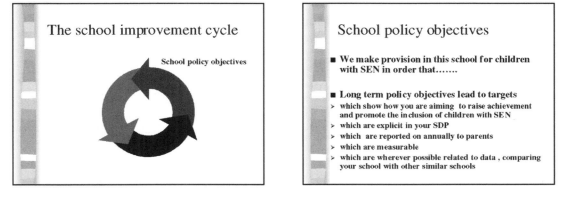

The school improvement cycle

School policy objectives

School policy objectives

- We make provision in this school for children with SEN in order that.......

- Long term policy objectives lead to targets
  > which show how you are aiming to raise achievement and promote the inclusion of children with SEN
  > which are explicit in your SDP
  > which are reported on annually to parents
  > which are measurable
  > which are wherever possible related to data, comparing your school with other similar schools

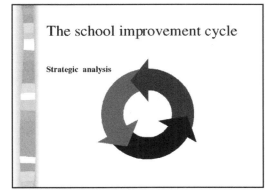

The school improvement cycle

Strategic analysis

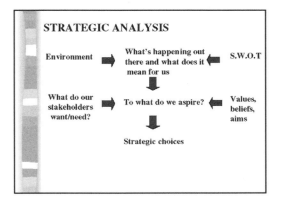

STRATEGIC ANALYSIS

Environment → What's happening out there and what does it mean for us ← S.W.O.T

What do our stakeholders want/need? → To what do we aspire? ← Values, beliefs, aims

Strategic choices

Strategic implications of national SEN policy

Key themes:
- school-based responsibilities
- early intervention
- pupil involvement
- parental involvement
- working in partnership with other agencies
- inclusion
- tackling disability discrimination

Strategic implications of national SEN policy

Key themes:
- focus on outcomes, raising standards, doing what works
- reducing bureaucracy and teacher workload
- importance of key transitions
- new roles for SENCO

Strategic implications of national SEN policy

- SEN seen as an interaction between the child and the school context
- SEN the job of every teacher
- LEAs have to make clear the provision the school is expected to make from its own resources
- The school holds the responsibility – emphasis on school action

Strategic implications of national SEN policy

Early intervention :
- identifying children's needs early on
- use of screening systems, and prioritising younger children when planning your provision

Strategic implications of national SEN policy

Parental involvement :
- parents as equal partners
- parent partnership schemes in every LEA
- greater role for parents in holding schools to account for the provision that they make for pupils with SEN

Strategic implications of national SEN policy

Pupil involvement :
- pupils have a right to be involved in making decisions and exercising choices
- we need to find ways of involving them in target setting and planning
- we must ascertain their views on all important decisions made about them

Strategic implications of national SEN policy

Working in partnership:

- expectation of integrated local services – health, education, social services
- school-based multiagency services to the local community

Strategic implications of national SEN policy

Inclusion:

- inclusion of pupils with SEN one aspect of a broader focus on inclusion for a range of vulnerable groups
- schools expected to change cultures, policies and practices
- new roles for special schools

Strategic implications of national SEN policy

All Statemented children must be educated in mainstream unless this is incompatible with :

- the wishes of the parent
- the efficient education of other children and there are no reasonable steps that can be taken to prevent incompatibility

Strategic implications of national SEN policy

It is unlawful for a school to discriminate against disabled pupils:

- in the education or associated services provided
- in admissions arrangements
- by excluding them from the school for reasons based on the disability

Schools' accessibility strategies must cover access to the curriculum (particularly written materials) as well as to the physical environment

Strategic implications of national SEN policy

Focus on outcomes, raising standards and doing what works:

- increased emphasis on schools exploiting best practice when choosing interventions
- expectation that outcomes will be defined and rates of progress measured

Strategic implications of national SEN policy

Reducing bureaucracy and teacher workload:

- IEPs only for provision that is additional to or different from the normal differentiated curriculum

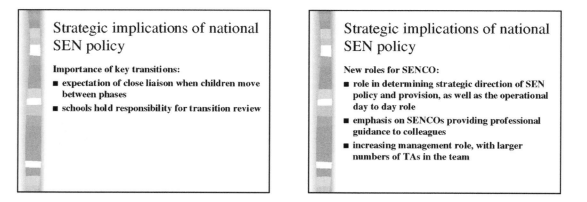

Strategic implications of national SEN policy

Importance of key transitions:

- expectation of close liaison when children move between phases
- schools hold responsibility for transition review

Strategic implications of national SEN policy

New roles for SENCO:

- role in determining strategic direction of SEN policy and provision, as well as the operational day to day role
- emphasis on SENCOs providing professional guidance to colleagues
- increasing management role, with larger numbers of TAs in the team

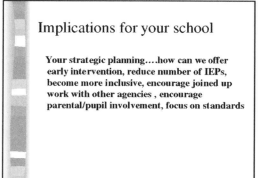

Implications for your school

Your strategic planning....how can we offer early intervention, reduce number of IEPs, become more inclusive, encourage joined up work with other agencies , encourage parental/pupil involvement, focus on standards

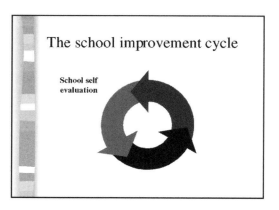

The school improvement cycle

School self evaluation

School self evaluation:why do it

- Because there's no point to all your hard work if it isn't helping children make progress
- Because if it is others can learn from you
- Because if it isn't you will want to change things
- Because it is important to new SENCO role
- Because OFSTED will be impressed

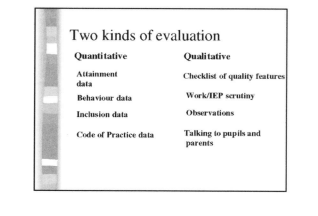

Two kinds of evaluation

Quantitative	Qualitative
Attainment data	Checklist of quality features
Behaviour data	Work/IEP scrutiny
Inclusion data	Observations
Code of Practice data	Talking to pupils and parents

Evaluating outcomes
Measuring rates of progress

Key question is:

- Do you have systems in place to find out if your provision is enabling pupils to make progress?
- Do you know how that progress compares with that made by children in other similar schools?

Value-added: individual pupil progress

- NC levels
- P levels
- Reading, spelling, maths standardised tests
- QCA behaviour scales

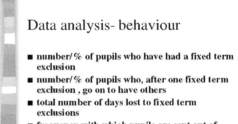

Absolute attainment of a cohort of pupils

- percentage of very low attainers at the end of each Key Stage
- percentage of children with SEN attaining nationally expected levels for the Key Stage

Data analysis- general

- Number of children moving down the levels of the Code of Practice - compared year on year

Data analysis - learning

- percentage of children attaining at least Level 1 (end KS1), Level 3 (end KS2), Level 4 (end KS3)
- percentage of children with SEN but without global learning difficulties attaining Level 2/4/5(according to your Key Stage)
- progress made over a Key Stage by children with below average starting points
- average gains on standardised tests of literacy/numeracy made by children receiving additional help

Data analysis- behaviour

- number/% of pupils who have had a fixed term exclusion
- number/% of pupils who, after one fixed term exclusion , go on to have others
- total number of days lost to fixed term exclusions
- frequency with which pupils are sent out of lessons to time out /withdrawal rooms/headteacher etc
- number/% of children on part time timetables

Data analysis - inclusion

- percentage of school population who leave to attend a special school or unit elsewhere
- number of pupils reintegrated from special school or unit placements elsewhere/ reintegrated following permanent exclusion from another school
- extent of social integration with the peer group for children with complex needs
- engaged time in the classroom for children with complex needs

Number of children at School Action, School Action Plus, with Statements

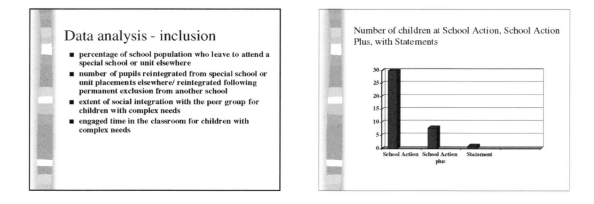

Numbers in a case study school

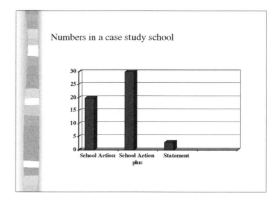

Two kinds of evaluation

Quantitative	Qualitative
Attainment data	Checklist of quality features
Behaviour data	Work/IEP scrutiny
Inclusion data	Observations
Code of Practice data	Talking to pupils and parents

Useful questions to ask yourself....

- How much time do subject coordinators in my school spend on lesson observation and work scrutiny?
- How much time does the SENCO spend?

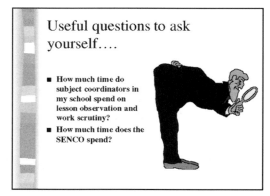

The school improvement cycle

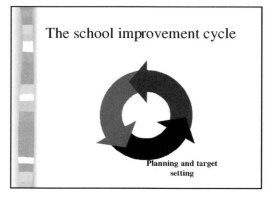

Planning and target setting

School development plans

- Measurable targets
- Strategies and actions
- Allocation of resources(tine and money)
- Interim measures or milestones
- Mechanisms for monitoring and evaluation – who will do what and when

The school improvement cycle

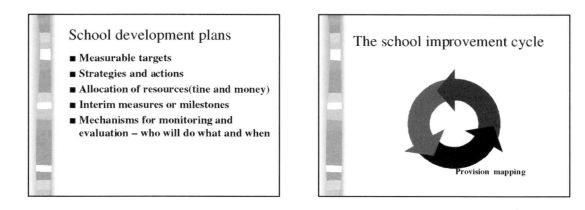

Provision mapping

Provision maps

		£
Year 7		
Year 8		
Year 9		

Planning provision :using a provision map

- Allows you plan provision
- Allows you to cost provision
- Allows you to make sure children don't get the same provision year after year

Costing your provision map

- In time
- In money
- What goes in - additional to and different from
- Costs of staffing, resources and equipment, purchasing from outside agencies, maintaining very small classes or sets

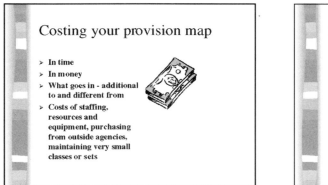

3 pieces in the jigsaw

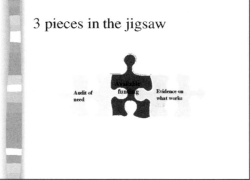

Audit of need   Available funding   Evidence on what works

What doesn't work?

- Diffuse LSA support
- Small reductions in class sizes
- Setting
- Expensive ICT schemes

What works

- Early intervention: nurture groups, social skills groups plus parenting support, early language and literacy intervention e.g Reading Recovery
- Acceleread/write , Phono-graphix, Catch-up, Better Reading Partnership, MTSR, Reciprocal teaching, Paired reading, THRASS
- Peer tutoring
- Social skills groupwork e.g. anger management
- Stress reduction
- Some mentoring schemes
- Some learning support units

The school improvement cycle

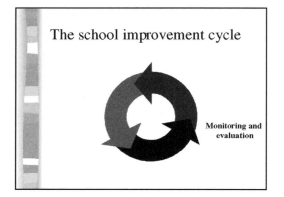

Monitoring and evaluation

Monitoring and evaluation

- Of *new* actions (school development plan)
- Of the quality and impact of the school's *ongoing* provision for children with SEN

Beating bureaucracy

...SEN can easily become a paper chase

...the way round this is to improve the inclusive provision that is normally available to all children , so as to reduce the numbers requiring something that is additional or different

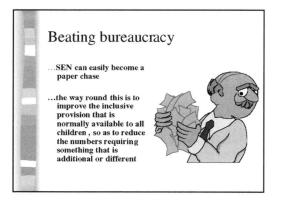

Why have we got so much bureaucracy?

- Stress on identifying individual children's needs
- Arranging and documenting provision for individuals so identified
- 40% rise in numbers identified in recent years

IEPs - the sacred cow?

- Numbers identified as having SEN - league tables
- Links to LEA funding
- Emphasis in Ofsted inspections
- Result - a shift in the focus away from teaching and learning, into attracting and maintaining funding via paperwork

A possible policy on when IEPs should be used

- For children with exceptional, truly individual needs
- When there is a sense of 'stuckness'
- When a multiagency response is needed

The school improvement cycle

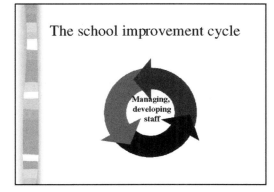

SENCO management and self management

- Self evaluation grid
- Self audit against national TTA SENCO standards
- Annual management cycle with performance targets

Role of SENCO

- Overseeing school policy
- Coordinating provision
- Liaising with and advising colleagues
- Managing LSAs (and teachers, in secondary)
- Overseeing record keeping
- Contributing to CPD of colleagues
- Liaising with parents
- Liaising with support services

Status and time required

- Equivalent to role of literacy, numeracy or curriculum coordinator…HOD or Head of Year
- Inappropriate to have other curriculum or (secondary) school-wide responsibilities
- 'Many schools find it appropriate for the SENCO to be a member of the senior management team'

Index